REWOVEN

Restoring God's Ultimate Design

Unraveling the Roots of Trauma
in the Life of the Believer

VICKI VIBBERT

Copyright

REWOVEN: Restoring God's Ultimate Design
Unraveling the Roots of Trauma in the Life of the Believer

Publisher: Book Breakthrough Publishing www.bookbreakthroughpublishing.com

ISBN:978-1-9996790-6-4

Table of Contents

Introduction

What is trauma?

Trauma, a word which has gained a lot of momentum in recent years, now packs a punch unlike in any other time in history. Words are powerful. They can bring hope, or they can bring defeat. They can bring understanding and yet in the wrong hands they can bring pain and confusion, which can leave a sting for years. Often this word is associated with those who have experienced a significant event such as rape, war, domestic violence or a natural disaster such as a fire, crime or a tornado.

While all of these events certainly are trauma inducing, the fact is that most of us have experienced some level of trauma throughout our lives, and as a result, we live trying to manage or hide its effects. If you've ever found yourself asking – "Why did I respond like that?", "What is wrong with me?" "Why can't I trust people?", "Will I ever feel normal?" or "Why am I so afraid, ashamed or disconnected?" then you are likely to have experienced trauma in your life. Many of these familiar questions have their roots in trauma responses. Trauma left unaddressed and unhealed can cause a myriad of responses, physically, emotionally and spiritually.

Perhaps your physical responses to trauma are what have driven you to take this course? Or, like many others, you may not be aware of what years of hidden grief and pain, or misunderstanding can do to even every cell in your body. Are you aware that we can now see markers of trauma on DNA? This means that we are even affected by the trauma in the genes of our family.

In the last two decades we have come to understand the devastating effects of trauma upon the body even on the cellular level. We now know that trauma affects the architecture of the brain, hormone levels, the nervous system as well as our immune systems. Many of the diseases and discomforts we struggle with are rooted not in disease, but in trauma. Perhaps in your journey, you have only identified the most common recognized effects such as headaches, depression or digestive irregularities.

DEVELOPMENTAL TRAUMA

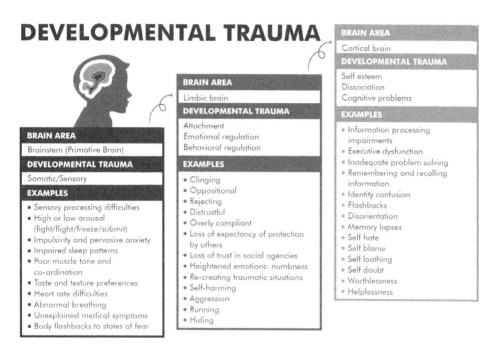

BRAIN AREA
Brainstem (Primitive Brain)

DEVELOPMENTAL TRAUMA
Somatic/Sensory

EXAMPLES
- Sensory processing difficulties
- High or low arousal (fight/flight/freeze/submit)
- Impulsivity and pervasive anxiety
- Impaired sleep patterns
- Poor muscle tone and co-ordination
- Taste and texture preferences
- Heart rate difficulties
- Abnormal breathing
- Unexplained medical symptoms
- Body flashbacks to states of fear

BRAIN AREA
Limbic brain

DEVELOPMENTAL TRAUMA
Attachment
Emotional regulation
Behavioral regulation

EXAMPLES
- Clinging
- Oppositional
- Rejecting
- Distrustful
- Overly compliant
- Loss of expectancy of protection by others
- Loss of trust in social agencies
- Heightened emotions: numbness
- Re-creating traumatic situations
- Self-harming
- Aggression
- Running
- Hiding

BRAIN AREA
Cortical brain

DEVELOPMENTAL TRAUMA
Self esteem
Dissociation
Cognitive problems

EXAMPLES
- Information processing impairments
- Executive dysfunction
- Inadequate problem solving
- Remembering and recalling information
- Identity confusion
- Flashbacks
- Disorientation
- Memory lapses
- Self hate
- Self blame
- Self loathing
- Self doubt
- Worthlessness
- Helplessness

Studies show that nearly 75% of all physical ailments and diseases find their roots in faulty thinking and biological responses to stress and turmoil. Our brain is a big organ and as such, it transmits impulses to every organ and nerve ending in our bodies. Emotional stress can cause nearly every disease imaginable. God spoke of this mystery in His Word repeatedly.

A cheerful heart is good medicine, but a crushed spirit dries up the bones.

Proverbs 17:22

Anxiety weighs down the heart, but a kind word cheers it up.

Proverbs 12:25

The soothing tongue is a tree of life, but a perverse tongue crushes the spirit.

Proverbs 15:4

A heart at peace gives life to the body, but envy rots the bones.

Proverbs 14:30

Gracious words are a honeycomb, sweet to the soul and healing to the bones.

Proverbs 16:24

And in Jesus' own words as the Great Physician, " The Spirit of the Sovereign Lord is upon me, because the Lord has anointed me to proclaim good news to the poor. He has sent me to bind up the brokenhearted, to proclaim freedom for the captives and release from darkness for the prisoners, to proclaim the year of the Lord's favor and the day of vengeance of our God, to comfort all who mourn and provide for those who grieve in Zion— to bestow on them a crown of beauty instead of ashes, the oil of joy instead of mourning, and a garment of praise instead of a spirit of despair."

Isaiah 61:1-3

Just as we address the lies that we believe in our mind as a result of our trauma and experiences, it is important to pray and allow the Holy Spirit to lead you in understanding areas of your body that have been affected by trauma. Your body keeps track of emotional events, just as your mind does. Latent emotions can be trapped in muscle memory or even your nervous system responses and organs.

Trauma is defined in multiple ways. It is the exposure to an event or a series of events which are emotionally harmful or life-threatening and which have a lasting effect on the person's functioning. You see trauma in a general sense can be ANYTHING that causes us to view God, ourselves or others through a lens of bondage. It sounds pretty broad and simplistic doesn't it? But it's true.

God created us to walk in freedom and in relationship with Himself, others and with ourselves. Anything less than that is bondage - a lack of freedom to be who and what He created us to be. God, the Creator of the universe, the Master Artist, the Master Weaver, created you in your mother's womb. He knew you and His primary purpose for your creation was for you to experience His love. Again, this sounds simplistic, doesn't it? But again, this is the truth. He longs to have relationship with you so that you may experience freedom.

That absent father = trauma.

That failed marriage = trauma.

Your child addicted to drugs = trauma.

Had a miscarriage or abortion = trauma

All of these and so many more are traumatic events which shape our view of self, our view of God and of others. But what about the more subtle events and issues like emotional entanglement, loss of boundaries, blaming, shaming, anger, rage, isolation and on and on? So many of these shape our everyday lives too, and yet we don't stop to realize that they are NOT what God has created for us.

With an increased understanding of neurological and biological responses to events in our past, the mental health community has developed a wide range of self-help and diagnostic means to determine "what is wrong with us." You see, we are the combination of the events that have shaped our lives and our responses to those events. Counseling and psychotherapy are readily available. Recovery and addiction support is just a "google" away, but yet we find ourselves in an era where society is still plagued with anxiety, guilt and depression.

Unlike the old adage that "knowledge is power," simply understanding our past is simply not enough to find lasting healing. Traditional therapy, support groups, addiction recovery, cognitive behavioral therapy, EMDR, brain spotting and drug therapies may all have their place, but until we address the spiritual components of trauma, we are left lacking. Simply modifying behavior is not the same as healing. Medicating does not bring healing and educating does not bring healing. True healing takes place when our BODY, SOUL and SPIRIT have all experienced freedom. We will cover these three key areas repeatedly throughout this course, so it's ok if it doesn't make sense to you right now.

Are you ready to do the work of placing yourself in the hands of the loving, caring, skilled Master Weaver? There may be some stretching to do and perhaps even some untying of knots and misplaced threads in your life. The process of healing isn't quick, and you may get frustrated along the way, as we can't always see the masterpiece that is being woven. This is because we sit on the underside, often seeing the

Simply modifying behavior is not the same as healing

mismatched colors, the knots and the frayed ends. It can be confusing, especially if we are only focused on one thread at a time. However, when we begin the process of submitting to the Weaver's master hand, we soon understand that the masterpiece He is weaving is us.

The following two poems both speak eloquently of the Master Weaver, an analogy that has been used for centuries. This first poem is often attributed to Corrie Ten Boom, although the actual author is unknown. She was a Holocaust survivor, not because she was Jewish, but because her family was imprisoned for running a safe house for many Jewish people. Her faith amidst her suffering is a beautiful testimony to what the Lord can do when we are truly submitted to His Weaving.

The second poem, written in the late 1800's, gives beautiful language to the "years of man, being the looms of God". This poem has been translated into multiple languages and is renowned in multiple poetic collections. Certainly, there are many analogies that one can draw from the weaving process, and we will touch on a few. However, regardless of the metaphorical usage, the purpose is to establish the understanding that trauma is a journey. It does have a beginning and with the Lord's help, it can also have an end.

"Life is but a Weaving"

Author Unknown

Quoted by Corrie ten Boom

My life is but a weaving
Between my God and me.
I cannot choose the colors
He weaveth steadily.
Oft' times He weaveth sorrow;
And I in foolish pride
Forget He sees the upper
And I the underside.
Not 'til the loom is silent
And the shuttles cease to fly
Will God unroll the canvas
And reveal the reason why.
The dark threads are as needful
In the weaver's skillful hand
As the threads of gold and silver
In the pattern He has planned
He knows, He loves, He cares;
Nothing this truth can dim.
He gives the very best to those
Who leave the choice to Him.
Corrie ten Boom

The Tapestry Weavers

By Anson G. Chester

*Let us take to our hearts a lesson—no lesson
can nobler be—*

*From the ways of the tapestry weavers on the
other side of the sea.*

*Above their heads the pattern hangs, they
study it with care,*

*And while their fingers deftly move, their eyes
are fastened there.*

*They tell this curious thing, besides, of the
patient, plodding weaver:*

*He works on the wrong side evermore but
works for the right side ever.*

*It is only when the weaving stops, and the web
is loosed and turned,*

*That he sees his real handiwork—that his
marvelous skill is learned.*

*Ah, the sight of its delicate beauty, how it pays
him for all his cost!*

*No rarer, daintier work than his was ever done
by the frost.*

*Then the master bringeth him golden hire, and
giveth him praise as well,*

And how happy the heart of the weaver is, no tongue but his can tell.

The years of man are the looms of God, let down from the place of the sun,

Wherein we are weaving ever, till the mystic web is done.

Weaving blindly but weaving surely each for himself his fate—

We may not see how the right side looks, we can only weave and wait.

But, looking above for the pattern, no weaver hath to fear.

Only let him look clear into heaven, the Perfect Pattern is there.

If he keeps the face of the Savior forever and always in sight

His toil shall be sweeter than honey, his weaving sure to be right.

And when the work is ended, and the web is turned and shown,

He shall hear the voice of the Master, it shall say unto him, "Well done!"

And the white-winged Angels of Heaven, to bear him shall come down.

And God shall give him gold for his hire—not a coin—but a glowing crown

ReWoven - Restoring God's Ultimate Design is not another Bible study or support group. It is designed to address the spiritual components of trauma and release freedom and true healing to many areas, where traditional modalities fall short.

Our intent is not to negate the need for counseling, drug therapies when appropriate, diet and health changes or support groups. Those practices can play a key component in your healing journey. But for many of us, we have been there and done that. You know there's more. You know there's true freedom. You want more than just slapping a religious bumper sticker on your pain and wearing the masks of perfection, perception and performance.

Knowledge, even biblical knowledge, falls short when not executed with the beautiful, powerful presence of the Holy Spirit, our Comforter. God, the Master Artist, created us in His image, three parts being. We must bring the presence of God to our body, soul and spirit, the three parts of man. The quoting of scripture, prayer, and meditating on His Word all have their important place, but until we encounter the presence of Jesus, we are often left with head knowledge, which has limited value and often leaves us relying on trite religious phrases and our own motivation to find healing. That is not the goal of this course. The intention of this writing will hopefully ring clearly throughout each word written and each exercise and accompanying class that is taught.

The work isn't always easy - it requires humility, vulnerability and courage. You may need some intensive heart work, or perhaps be willing to uncover a hidden pain or wounding that you've never shared, but the effects of which have infected every part of your emotional being. You may have to take responsibility for some mistakes and woundings you have caused others. There may be attitudes of victimization, shame or control that now will need to be pulled out, thread by thread to replace them with cords of righteousness and truth. The Master Weaver is ready. He's been ready, steadily weaving a masterpiece......YOU!

Let the Weaving Begin.......

> *" The Spirit of the Lord is on me, because he has anointed me to proclaim good news to the poor. He has sent me to proclaim freedom for the prisoners and recovery of sight for the blind, to set the oppressed free."*
>
> *Luke 4:18.*

How to get the most out of this book and workbook

Healing is a journey. You may find that some chapters are much more work intensive depending on your individual background. It is crucial that you spend time with the Lord and allow him to reveal and speak to you about areas that He desires to touch. There is simply no substitute for time spent with Him, particularly If you have never addressed areas of trauma in your life.

It is advisable to read the chapter early in the week and work through the workbook in stages, as the week allows. This will allow you to process the material. You may also find it helpful to utilize the short devotional teachings which accompany each chapter. It is easy to assume that something doesn't apply individually if you do not take the time to assess your heart condition and proceed with vulnerability.

If you have not done the preparation work of the week before class, it will be difficult to receive the prayer ministry that follows as your heart will not have been plowed and prepared...the soil must be tilled. If you are having difficulty with the subject matter or feel that you are being triggered, remember to reach out to your mentor or class coach.

While the analogies in ReWoven all speak to the process of a tapestry being woven by the Master Weaver, no expert knowledge of the weaving process is necessary. However, the following terms are used frequently throughout the text and workbook and should serve as a guide for application.

| Burling

This is the removal of loose threads, knots, slubs, burrs, and other extraneous material from fabrics, before finishing without damaging them, by using a burling iron or tweezers. A burl is a small knot or lump in a thread or fabric.

How this applies to your Master Weaver and you: lies and thematic trauma create knots, and burrs in the beautiful fabric that our Master Weaver designed for us to be.

| Bleeding

This refers to colors which run together from wet, dyed material onto a material next to it — the colors 'bleed' onto each other. It has been known that the property of bleeding is sometimes caused through the use of fugitive dyes or through bad dyeing techniques.

How this applies to your Master Weaver and you: when we have wounds, they can 'bleed' onto the lives and psyche of others as well as onto other relationship areas in our lives.

| Blending

This is a process which involves combining two or more types of staple fibres in one yarn to achieve a 'blend' or mixture of either two types of natural fibre, a natural fibre with a man-made fibre or several colored fibres, therefore achieving a color mixture.

How this applies to your Master Weaver and you: emotional or physical enmeshment with another person we are or have been in relationship with, creates a soul tie which can be detrimental to us. A part of who they are and their traits can become 'blended' with our personality – and we become, in part, like them and they like us.

A 'good' soul tie is the result of a godly, holy relationship but a bad one the result of a toxic, ungodly or unhealthy relationship without good boundaries.

| Batten

This is a weaving tool designed to push the weft yarn securely into place.

How this applies to your Master Weaver and you: When you apply the 'batten' to your life – your mind and soul – you are applying personal truth into the tapestry of your life, which is life changing for you and serves to 'rewire' and renew your mind.

| Perch

This is the name for a machine or wooden frame over which a fabric is inspected for faults, illuminated from behind by natural or artificial light.

How this applies to your Master Weaver and you: Allow the Holy Spirit to be your 'perch' – to highlight the areas that He desires to touch and purify.

| Scour

This is the name for the process of scouring. This involves washing all types of textile fibres, yarn or cloth to remove dirt, natural fats, waxes, proteins, oil or other impurities.

How this applies to your Master Weaver and you: When we 'scour', we are going through the process of repentance which allows us to receive healing and to be 'washed' as white as snow.

| Sleyhook

This is a small flat tool with a hook on one or both ends, which is used to pull warp ends through the reed. This is an essential weaving tool.

How this applies to your Master Weaver and you: 'Sleying the hook' refers to the ability to grab "a lie" that you have identified that you are believing and pull it out or through the rest of the tapestry, so that it no longer affects you.

| Warping

This is the preparation of a number of threads (ends) which are arranged in order, number and width, parallel to each other and wound on the back beam on the loom.

How this applies to your Master Weaver and you: this is the framework upon which the tapestry of your life is woven. This represents the established truths and early structure of our lives which form a framework upon which we build our beliefs, thoughts and actions.

| Warp and weft

These are the two basic components used in weaving to turn the thread or yarn into fabric. The lengthwise yarns are held in tension on the loom while the horizontal weft is drawn through and inserted over and under the warp.

How this applies to your Master Weaver and you: Too much tension in our lives can cause damage to who we are and result in us experiencing trauma, which if unaddressed, affects every aspect of our life and relationships from then on.

01

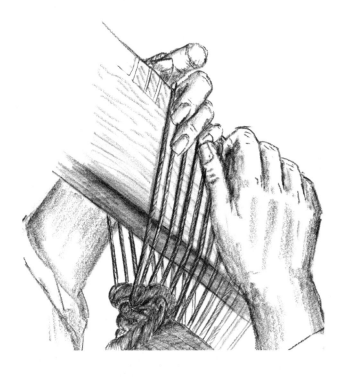

Chapter 01

Warping the Loom

Imagine for a moment the Master Weaver, sitting quietly contemplating every thread, color and texture in His Hands, creating a mystery picture that is only revealed at its culmination. One does not have to be a master weaver to see the obvious spiritual analogies present in the process. The preparation of the loom is as important as the weaving process itself. The careful artist secures the vertical threads in preparation with just the right amount of tension to withstand the constant stretching and movement that will occur. This process of preparation is called "warping the loom".

For those of us not familiar with such a term, the word 'warp' can certainly create an altogether different image in our minds. Warp are the vertical yarns attached to the loom, and although instructions vary depending on the size and type of loom that is being used, the purpose is the same – to hold the loom steady for the process. Just as we are prepared for adulthood by the influences and experiences we have as children, warping occurs in our lives. If done with the right amount of tension, for instance our parents give us love but firm boundaries, then our preparation stage sets us up well to withstand the stretching of difficult circumstances in later years.

But if not, then the warping process takes on a different meaning – one reminiscent of our usual association with the word 'warp'. In contrast to gentle weaving, if the 'warping' we received as children was fraught with too much tension, it results in something that is broken or stretched out of its original form. And there we have our first metaphor for trauma.

Trauma stretches us out or away from our original form. We aren't broken, but we are wounded. Wounds can heal with time and with the right medicine or procedures. Certainly, there are times we may feel "warped" or stretched out of place. Often when working with children who have experienced trauma, you will hear people say, **"What's wrong with them, that they.....?"** You can then fill in the blank with whatever behavior is causing someone to ask that question.

Famed psychiatrist, Bruce Perry, author of "The Boy Who Was Raised as a Dog", has begun changing the narrative around this faulty question and reframing it as **"What happened to them that they behave in such a manner?"** This simple adjustment of the question reframes how we view those who have experienced trauma.

We are all the result of the events and experiences of our lives, as well as our responses to those events and experiences. When we look at people through the eyes of a trauma informed response, we are not giving license for poor behavior or negative choices. We are, however, laying a framework which removes shame and allows us to unravel the negative and causative events that have shaped this person's experience.

The warp of your personal loom is undoubtedly very different from anyone else in the room with you at this time. Every aspect of your life, such as where you were born, your birth order, your socioeconomic status, your education, your exposure to God, and the stability or lack thereof in your home all work and weave together to create the grid around which everything else is woven. You may have had wealth, extended family support and a great school, but if your father was an alcoholic behind closed doors, a couple of those warps are not secure. This is the understanding that we need to have – that everything in our background affects how we react and even perceive trauma.

We will look at our basic framework to determine the general areas of trauma that may be present before we look at specific or event focused trauma. Because the word trauma has such a strong connotation, we will often address the areas we are looking at with the phrase, "Lies I have believed". Not all lies are traumatic, however, when they are interwoven throughout the fabric of our lives undetected, they draw focus from the overall pattern or picture that is being woven. Other more obvious lies literally introduce the wrong threads into our tapestry, which need to be removed by a 'sleying hook' lest they falsely color our design.

If you're already thinking, "Well my life has had some rough spots, but I'm not sure I'd label it as trauma?" try asking yourself this question: "Is your relationship with God, yourself and others at peace or do you know that there are areas that are clouded by misperceptions and likely lies?" That is the area of your trauma. We are not unraveling trauma to keep you stuck in it, or even to give you tools to manage it. The goal is to honestly look at the tapestry of our lives and determine where there are knots, missing threads, and/or distorted pictures and blemishes – those black marks on our soul from past hurts.

*Past hurts can become black marks on
the beautiful tapestry of our lives*

No doubt trauma is subjective. If you are able to identify an event or series of events as distressing, you likely are able to connect with the word *trauma*. However, if you've been taught or have picked up a variety of coping mechanisms and never identified those disturbing and distressing events as trauma, then you are likely negating the seriousness of what has occurred in your past. We are in no way attaching a label of victimization to your experiences, for we are more than conquerors through Christ Jesus, but we cannot be victorious over what we have not yet named.

When trauma becomes normalized due to such things as cultural or religious norms, we can easily distance ourselves from the depths of pain which were experienced. Let's correct a few of those WARP(ed) ways of thinking so that the framework we are allowing God to weave on is based in truth and able to sustain the Weaver's touch.

01   Being exposed to drug or alcohol addiction at a young age is not normal

02   Being exposed to sexual activity or images at a young age is not normal

03   It is not normal to go to the funeral of your child

04   It is not normal to be touched in a sexual manner as a child

05   It is not normal to be hit, kicked, slapped or physically abused

06   It is not normal to be berated and screamed at

07   It isn't normal to go through the remains of your home after a tornado, fire, flood or a burglary

08   It isn't normal to raise yourself or your siblings

09   It is not normal to be abandoned by a parent

10   It is not normal to be homeless

This is just the beginning of the warping that can occur when we believe that what we've experienced is "normal". We deny the impact of trauma and can often have misplaced guilt, anger or fear as a result of not correctly addressing the causative and formative events in our early years.

Misplaced anger turned inward is the result of a life infiltrated with trauma and is a common reaction to unresolved and unrecognized trauma. Many people live their entire lives on a constant roller coaster of reactivity. The fact that you are beginning that journey is a tremendous step toward your healing and your breaking the cycle of generational trauma in your life.

Time alone does not heal trauma

Time alone does not heal trauma. Faith alone does not heal trauma, neither does traditional talk therapy. Medicine, though necessary at times, may camouflage healing and living our lives typically adds more trauma. So where do we start? We've acknowledged that we are "warped", so now it's time to look at the framework of the loom. We are in position to allow the Weaver to take His position.

Our Framework

Our earliest childhood experiences create a framework upon which the weaving process begins. Our framework of understanding as well as the framework of our composition is important in the process of how we adapt and respond to trauma. The warping is attached directly to the framework. Depending on your age, gender, personality, and choices, the way in which the warping affects your "framework" may be drastically different to that of someone else who experienced the exact same type of event. Trauma is based both in PERCEPTION and REALITY. We can be traumatized due to our perception of an event, even if the actual facts of the situation are vastly different from what we believe.

The type of yarn used for warping is to be smooth and able to withstand the tension, without giving way and is also able to hold the tapestry to its true form.

These strong yarn fibers must hold the form of the tapestry. This framework is what the enemy attempts to destroy through trauma.

Our spiritual framework is built around **identity, purpose and connection.** When these threads are missing or weakened, the tapestry is no longer true to its proposed form. Psalm 139:13 reads "For you created my innermost parts, You wove me together in my mother's womb." When our identity is lost, our purpose hidden, and our connection non-existent, we are left with the distortions of a life marked with **fear, rejection and isolation.**

As we will discuss throughout this curriculum, the role of the enemy is to break relationship between you and your Heavenly Father. He begins attacking you as a child to shake your identity and framework because he knows who and what you are called to be. He is scheming against your identity, purpose and calling long before you are likely aware of any of those things.

One of the most common ways the enemy seeks to destroy your relationship with God is by attacking the character and nature of God. These lies create frustration, disappointment, anger and often a crisis of faith completely. If we do not have a framework upon which the identity, nature and character of God are secure, then we will not be able to withstand the "warping" of the enemy.

Trauma can cause one to ask some of the most difficult questions spiritually:

01   Why do bad things happen to good people?

02   Where was God when I was hurt, abused or abandoned?

03   Did I do something wrong that I deserve this?

04   Why do some people experience such hell, while others don't?

We cannot rightfully address trauma without at least giving a basis for all of these pressing questions. We must start with what we know to be true. God is GOOD. His nature and love are everlasting and not fickle. Giving trite responses to someone's trauma such as "It must have been God's will," or "He will use this to make you stronger" are NOT representative of a loving God. Trauma and pain are not caused by God....period. It is not His nature. Trauma is caused by sin and the fallen nature of man and the world.

God's plan is for redemption. His sacrifice upon the cross was so that we could freely choose to accept Him. It would not be a free choice if we were puppets that had to obey and choose Him for that is control. It is within that place of free will that mankind and the world chooses whom they will serve and because we are a part of that world, we do at times reap the consequences of those choices, both those of others as well as those of our own.

> Finding purpose in your suffering or experience is not what God designed for you. Do not get twisted in that religious lie. He may use your overcoming to produce a purpose or anointing that may not have been there had you not walked through your pain, but do not lay hold of the lie that He caused or purposed your trauma. He is not the origin of your pain.

He can however take frayed yarns, knotted threads and even ugly colors and weave them into a story which is redemptive and beautiful if we allow it. Some of you may already know how your trauma has given you insight into helping others or placed you on a career or spiritual path that you would have otherwise not been drawn to. Just as Jesus's scars told an incredible story, so do yours.

It is important before we move forward that if you have embraced any of the lies about God and his nature that we address those, for they will surely lay a snare to receiving truth as we move forward. Ask God to show you any area where you have believed a lie about God's love and purpose for your life. Write these down and we will revisit this in an upcoming chapter.

Can you identify ways in which you have mischaracterized the nature of God? Are you holding God responsible for wounds that man inflicted? Can you see the twisting of the enemy's craftiness in that lie?

Are you angry with the Weaver?

It is not uncommon for people to become resentful, angry or even untrusting when trauma has been a component of their life. Unfortunately, these lies create distance and a breakdown of relationship between you and your Heavenly Father. All too often the church gives a sympathetic, although not Biblical response of saying, "It's ok, go ahead and yell and scream at God. He can take it". While certainly the Creator of the universe does not wince any more at our temper tantrums than He did at those of Job, it does affect our relationship with Him and gives legal right to the enemy to torment us.

When we blame God for our suffering, doubt His care, rage and throw our fists in the air, we have entered into a realm of judgment of God and His nature

When we blame God for our suffering, doubt His care, rage and throw our fists in the air, we have entered into a realm of judgment of God and His nature. How can we simultaneously ask for Him to heal us if subconsciously or even blatantly we blame Him? The emotion and confusion that arises as the result of trauma is natural, but it is the positioning of our heart stance and how we approach God that is critical to our healing journey.

When we are angry with a person it implies a strong sense of disapproval. If you are angry with me, you believe I have done something wrong. This is where we get into error with God. We are not the judge. It is arrogant and even foolish to believe we can stand in judgment of God.

"Far be it from you to do such a thing- to kill the righteous with the wicked, treating the righteous and the wicked alike. Far be it from you! Will not the Judge of all the earth do right?"

Gen 18:25

This certainly does not imply that we stuff what we are feeling or become hypocritical for denying what we may feel. If you are experiencing anger or resentment at God, take it to Him and ask Him to reveal truth and unravel the entanglement. Being honest about emotion is fine. However, it is NOT ok when we position ourselves in judgment of God's actions or what He permits. Often when one says it is ok to be angry with God, what they are really trying to say is that it is ok to express anger. Let us define the difference then: it is entirely different to express anger to God in contrast to expressing anger at God.

Saying, "God, I feel so angry. I feel abandoned at a time that I really needed to feel You", is different from yelling at God in a tirade, accusing Him of betraying you. These types of judgment on the character and nature of God can thwart our healing because it creates a barricade that separates us from the tangible presence of God. It doesn't change that He is there, but it certainly can affect our ability to feel Him.

Remember when Jesus felt alone on the cross, suffering the most grueling of physical and emotional trauma? He cried out, "My God, My God, where are you?" He acknowledged his human emotion of feeling alone. He was not raging at God, but rather taking His pain, questions and circumstances to God. Moments later He cried out, "Into Your hands, I commit my spirit."

All too often when counseling with an individual, we will find them stuck in their journey, truly wanting to move forward but unable to be free from the lies that torment them. All too often the open door or open invitation to the enemy's torment is a hidden judgment or resentment of God. Unraveling these foundational issues is an intrinsic part of establishing the framework upon which the Master Weaver can begin the healing process. The foundation that God is good, just, merciful and kind.

Just as it is vitally important to understand the true nature of God, so we must also be aware of the nature of our enemy. We are to be alert to his devices. When we correctly understand him and his nature, then we can properly discern the false from the true.

The nature of the enemy

We have discussed the nature of God and the nature of man, but now, we must take a look at the nature of the enemy. Satan's fall from the presence of God positioned him to forever be the accuser of the brethren. That's right....his total, consuming job is to bring accusation against you and present it to the Father. He does this by lying to you about the nature and character of God, your own nature and often the nature of others. These lies open the doors or wrap around events in our lives that cause us to doubt salvation, personal worth or even a hope for a future.

In Matthew 4 Satan offers Jesus the kingdoms of the world. These kingdoms are both geographical and governmental. Satan leads a hierarchy of demonic beings that have authority in this world. In level II we will deal at length with the role of the demonic with regard to trauma, but for now, acknowledging that there is a war, and you are on the battlefield is essential. Knowing your enemy is a prime strategy for victory.

James 4:7 Says,

"Submit yourselves, then, to God. Resist the Devil, and he will flee from you."

We cannot resist what we do not identify. The problem is we often don't recognize the voice we are heeding is the voice of the enemy, not our own, and certainly not the voice of Father God. We will spend much time throughout the course learning to identify the accusations of the enemy. We will apply the sleyhook to pull them from the very threads and fibers of our experiences.

Satan longs to destroy relationship - your relationship with yourself and others but ultimately the most important one of all - your relationship with God the Father. He is not only attacking you in the present and harassing you with lies from the past, but he is attacking your future. He knows the plans and purposes God has for you. He knows your spiritual DNA. No wonder much of what has been targeted at you is the direct result of the enemy's plans to thwart your destiny and calling.

Perch and Scour

Jesus, I acknowledge that sometimes I confuse my voice or the voice of the enemy with your voice. Help me to grow in the truth of who You are - your character and nature. Help me to recognize the areas where I accuse You of things that are contrary to Your nature, that belong at the feet of the enemy.

Father, if there are lies I am believing about You or myself, please help those to rise to the surface so that I can bring them into the truth of Your light. Father, help me to find security in the promises of who You are and Your love for me. I know that in You alone lies the only place that I can find true healing. So many times, I believe the voices that swirl around in my head or the accusations that are hurled from others. Help me to bring these into balance with who You say that I am.

Jesus, as I begin this journey of healing I give You permission to touch the painful and hidden places of my heart. I give You permission to uncover the hidden threads and loosen the knots. I trust You as the Weaver of my tapestry.

I give You permission to uncover the hidden threads and loosen the knots

02

Chapter 02

The Master Weaver:
In HIS image

Weaving is an ancient practice that has been used by people groups for centuries, yet its process is seemingly unchanged, although modernized by machinery in some areas. We addressed in chapter one the importance of the warp being tethered to the framework. When we look at the actual process of weaving, it is built on the word 'darn' which comes from the French word "to mend". For most of us older than thirty, we likely remember a parent or grandparent "darning" a pair of socks. It is possible now to order a small compact darning loom for such a purpose, although the traditional way of just using a darning needle will also work for those holey socks nestled in our drawers.

The basic process of darning is simple enough. You anchor the thread in the fabric on the edge of the hole and carry it across the gap. You then use a blanket stitch to provide strength and covering by a series of right angles. The spiritual metaphors in this process are many. The holes are representative of the trauma we have experienced that has left gaps in our life and brokenness where love or belonging was missing. The course for healing requires us to be securely anchored to our original God given image. The stolen or ripped threads must be replaced by truth to provide covering and protection of the original form. Even the correlation with the stitches being at a 90-degree angle speaks to the plumbline or truth found only in Christ. When we base our weaving on worldly philosophies and self-help materials, we often distort the original intended design, even from our well-meaning desire to repair a "hole."

Understanding that we are a tri-part being, created in the image of God, is essential in making sure that our process of repair and healing is truly anchored in God's identity and not a self-made or worldly imposed, counterfeit version.

God is a God of patterns. Throughout scripture God lays a framework upon which certain principles are laid over and over again. He does it by building precept upon precept. By understanding these patterns and principles, we defend ourselves against creating "cherry picked" doctrines or practices. For a doctrine to be true, it must be true in the entirety of scripture. It must be as true in Ecuador, Iran and China as it is in the United States.

We do not want to conform scripture to our cultural understandings of how God moves, speaks or even what He says in His Word. Understanding the patterns lets us define the character and nature of God, of man and of the enemy. Many of the struggles we face in life are a direct reflection of not understanding one or all of these roles. Do you believe God is a punishing taskmaster? Believe you are unworthy of love and forgiveness? Believe the devil is a red-faced being with a pitchfork who sits on your shoulder? All of these lies are tied up in not understanding the nature and character of God, man and the enemy. When we begin to unravel these mysteries, we unlock truth for healing, redemption and regaining control of our journey.

We could write an entire book on the patterns of God and actually several have, but for our purposes in this curriculum, we are going to look closely at the pattern of God and man. It is no mistake that scripture says, "God created mankind in his own image," Genesis 1:27. The 'trinity" is a concept that came out of man's desire to explain the complex nature of God. Early Church Father Tertullian first introduced this term in 213 AD. It was later adopted as official church doctrine at the council of Nicea, a century later in 325 AD. You won't find the word in scripture, but the basis for this explanation is plentiful. The patterns and examples of God, Jesus and Holy Spirit are throughout the whole of the Old and New Testament. At its deepest truth there still lies a mystery, because He is God, and well.....we aren't.

Scripture tells us that man was made in God's image. Well, what does that mean? God is a tri-part being. God the Father, God the Son and God the Holy Spirit. They are separate functions yet are all part of the Godhead. If it seems as though that we are simplifying a very complex concept, it is being done on purpose. The doctrinal understanding of the Trinity is far less important at this juncture than understanding the pattern and prototype.

This pattern of **THREE in ONE** is seen in God's design of man as well.

Man has a **Spirit** - where he communes with God

Man has a **Soul** - where he communes with others and self

Man has a **Body** - where he communes with the outside world

I am a SPIRIT, who has a SOUL, who lives in a BODY.

Understanding the role of our spirit and soul is key to growing in maturity and discipleship, but it is also key to finding lasting healing. As we will discuss throughout this course, we cannot rationalize or simply "educate" ourselves out of the effects of trauma. We can't even just repent the trauma away. When we begin to understand what it means to have our spirit rule OVER our soul, we begin to see the pattern of authority which was established in the Godhead. By submitting our soul to the authority of our spirit man, we are able to bring lies and wounding into submission to ultimate truth and freedom. We must allow the tangible presence of God's Spirit to touch us and remove the lies that enter through events, sins and wrong beliefs.

Scripture goes to great lengths to break down the understanding of flesh and spirit. You will find though that mainly due to transitions and the language barriers, there are times when "soul and spirit" are used interchangeably.

The Bible teaches that we consist of **body, soul and spirit:** Paul tells us in Thessalonians, "May your whole spirit, soul and body be preserved blameless at the coming of our Lord Jesus" (I Thessalonians 5:23). Our material bodies are visible to us, but our souls and spirits are less distinguishable and live in the invisible realm.

The Tri-part Nature of Man

Our soul is the part of us where much of the battle is fought, and the spirit is where much of the battle is won. Let's examine this more. The soul is composed again of three parts: our **Mind, Will** and **Emotions.**

This is one of the most important concepts you will need to grasp as we refer to it repeatedly throughout this course. Just as there is a divine hierarchy and authority structure to the Godhead, there should in turn be a hierarchy and authority structure to the trinity of man. God the Father is in authority over Jesus as well as the Holy Spirit. Remember when Jesus in John 5:19 says, *"Verily I truly say to you, the Son can do nothing by himself; he can only do what he sees his Father do."* Just as Jesus is in submission to the Father, so must we learn to bring the SOUL under the submission of the SPIRIT. This means our mind, will and our emotions can and should be brought under the reign of the Holy Spirit. The same is true of our body.

Just as Jesus is in submission to the Father, so must we learn to bring the SOUL under the submission of the SPIRIT

This simple and yet divine and complex teaching can literally change everything about how you view God, the world and yourself. For too long the church has allowed intellect and or emotion to rule instead of diligently teaching true discipleship which allows people to strengthen their "inner man" and find true deliverance and freedom. We are not slaves to our emotions, thoughts and our intellect, but if we do not know how to take authority over our own SOUL.....it will indeed reign. Be aware also that if you are the type of personality who tends to rely on your intellect, you may too quickly assume that you do not struggle in this area of understanding. Remember the MIND is also a key component of the soul. Logic and reason, without spirit, is just as out of balance as being ruled by emotion.

Let's pull these apart in a little more depth.

| Spirit -

In the Old Testament, the word *ruach* occurs 377 times. It is often translated as "wind or breath or spirit." The spirit or breath of a person returns to God at the time of death, and the body returns to dust. The Greek word 'pneuma' is used throughout the New Testament as "spirit or breath". It is interesting to contrast the creation of man with the death of man. When God created Adam from dust, He then breathed 'ruach' or breath into him. At death, the spirit returns to God, and the body then returns to the earth.

| Soul -

Nephesh is the Hebrew word for soul, occurring 755 times. It is translated in a myriad of ways depending on its context. The most common translation is "life" or "person". In the New Testament the word used is 'psuche', with similar translations.

Ps. 23:3

Matt 26:38

Heb 4:12

| Body -

In Hebrew, the body is referred to as '*basar*' and in Greek, the term 'sarx' is used. It is used when describing animals or physical parts of humans. It is used to contrast material things with spiritual things, as in Jer 17:5 and Matt 16:17. It is often described as being carnal, or not spiritually minded. This is again where we see the interception of body and soul being different from the spirit.

Paul references this in Romans 7:18 where he says, "For I know that good itself does not dwell in me, that is, in my sinful nature. For I have the desire to do what is good, but I cannot carry it out."

There is intentionality in the way in which scripture breaks down the body, soul and spirit. This design is not accidental or extraneous doctrine. It is intrinsic to our ability and our understanding of walking in the Spirit. This often-used Christianese term is often confused with the concept of utilizing spiritual gifts, which is wholly different from being in the spirit or a better way of phrasing it would be to be allowing our spirit to rule over our soul.

The Process of Salvation

Paul addresses this when he explains that we were saved (our spirit), we are being saved (our soul), and we will be saved (our body).

We are saved - **justification**. This is our spirit.

We are being saved - **sanctification**. This is our soul — our mind, will and emotions.

We shall be saved - **glorification**. This is our body.

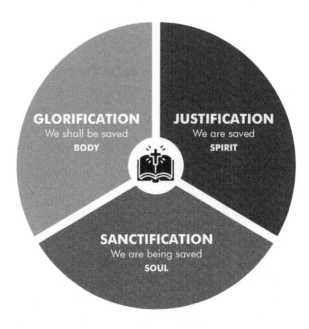

God uses the number 3 throughout scripture to refer to completeness. It is certainly not circumstantial that the process of salvation is divided into 3 states. When we accept Christ, our spirit is indwelt with the presence of the Holy Spirit. We receive fully the "gift" of salvation that is based solely on the death of Christ. It is unmerited and full of grace. The word "justification" means to show something to be right or to declare it to be righteous. When we accept the gift of salvation we are declared to God as righteous based on the sacrifice or blood covering of Jesus.

The second stage of our salvation is the process by which we grow in the nature and stature of Christ. This sanctification process means to be set apart for special use or purpose. This is the path of discipleship and also the path of healing. Step by step we sanctify our mind, will and emotions to the victory that Christ already won for us. By aligning and submitting these wounds, desires and beliefs to the authority of our spirit, which has already been saved....we see the gift of that salvation take root in our lives.

The final stage comes at our death and is known as glorification. When we die, we receive a new "body." Some would argue that it is not a body at all but an altogether new spiritual state. Regardless of your belief, the physical body that we have here becomes altogether new and healed.

Our spirit is indwelt with the Spirit of God when we accept Him as Savior. We spend the rest of our days laying down or crucifying our flesh (soul) to allow our Spirit to reign. Finally, upon our death or our bodily resurrection, our bodies are made whole once again as well.

1 Thessalonians 5:23 tells us, "May God himself the God of peace sanctify you through and through. May your whole spirit, soul and body be kept blameless at the coming of our Lord Jesus Christ.."

This sanctification happens as He saturates our whole being, starting with our spirit. He then works on our soul and eventually our bodies.

1 Corinthians 2:14-15 Paul writes, " The person without the Spirit does not accept the things that come from the spirit of God but considers them foolishness, and cannot understand them because they are discerned only through the Spirit. The person with the Spirit makes judgments about all things, but such a person is not subject to merely human judgments."

There is opposition between the spiritual part of us and our soul

There is opposition between the spiritual part of us and our soul. The spirit of man comes directly from the spirit of God. The rebellion in the garden occurred when man set aside his spirit and allowed his soul to be in control. God's desire is to reestablish the proper order in which the spirit rules over the soul and body.

The ability to understand spiritual things is dependent on the spirit. When the soul is not in direct submission to the spirit, the ways of the soul will rule, and spiritual discernment is lost. Our soul must be submitted to our spirit and our spirit must be in communion with God. But there is always tension between the soul and the spirit.

Throughout the New Testament, the same Greek word for "soulish" is translated in a myriad of ways: natural, sensual, worldly, without the spirit, following their natural instinct. When our soul is in control, we can see different manifestations such as:

01   The inability to perceive God's voice due to our own will and choices

02   Getting stuck in a place of intellectual pride or false doctrine

03   Instability and chaos rule as we are always at the whim of our emotional response

04   Rollercoaster relationship with God

05   The tendency to view things through the lens of a religious spirit

06   Gravitation toward looking for spiritual experiences

But what does THIS have to do with trauma? Putting it simply, everything.

For too long, therapeutic modalities have addressed our intellectual understanding of trauma. There are so many types of therapy: cognitive behavior therapy, talk therapy, regression therapy and many, many more. In the realm of the body, there are physiological components of trauma such as nutritional deficiencies, adrenal issues, genetic components or substituting one type of addiction for another with an idolatry of physical fitness, eating plans or massage and more. Again, we never want to convey that these options may not have some benefit.

What we are attempting to explain though is that the spiritual component of healing is often neglected or omitted altogether. Often when a faith component of counseling is addressed, it is simply from the standpoint of "finding community or acknowledging a "higher power" in your life". If that is what you are looking for, please stop and ask yourself if you really think that another support group to talk through your pain, or saying a prayer to a "higher power" will bring life changing healing? We think you will agree that the answer is unfortunately NO.

Soul Work

So where do we start the process of bringing our soul under the submission of our spirit? We start with our emotions. First of all, they are not trustworthy and in fact when unbridled, they can be destructive. This is where the personal work begins. When we understand that what we "feel" isn't always true, we start to unveil where the root of much trauma may lie.

If we allow our emotions to rule over us, instead of our spirit, we will always be subject to circumstances or to others. It's time to begin to diagnose those things in our lives that elicit strong emotional responses. A really good place to start is to ask yourself, "When do I overreact or when is my reaction out of balance with the event, comment or situation at hand?"

Being devastated emotionally due to the death of a loved one is valid. Being devastated because your husband didn't put the dishes away....not so much. This is also where some humility and honest evaluation can be really helpful. Do you have people in your life who can speak truth to you? Ask them, "When do you see me overreacting to situations?" Please note that we are not addressing trauma triggers such as smells, events, or visual stimuli that elicit strong panic responses. We will address this type of trauma response in a later chapter.

Start asking yourself these questions:

01   Why did I respond that way?

02   Am I in control of my emotions, or do my emotions rule over me?

03   How do I process intense emotion?

04   Do my emotions cause other behaviors like self-harm, drinking, sexual sin, binge eating, or over-spending?

The pattern is the blueprint for the image. When the pattern gets distorted, the image is blurred, damaged or even lost. Consequently, weavers will place the pattern above them on the ceiling where they can rightly follow the gridwork for the design. We too must look up in submission to our Creator to see the image that He is creating for it is built on a pattern of becoming like Him. This requires continual submission of our mind, will and emotions so that we are able to live in constant communion with Him. Understanding the pattern of body, soul and spirit allows us to see the ways in which the image is attacked through lies and

We were created to have a beautiful pattern made up of body, soul and spirit unfettered and unblemished by trauma

events. These distortions separate us from the original design of communion with God. He so longs to establish harmony and restore broken relationship with you where this distortion has torn at the very fibers of your design. So many believers who have experienced trauma doubt the love, presence and character of God. That is the plan of the enemy, deceiving us into believing that the blemishes and distortions were actually placed there by the Creator instead of by the fallen nature of man and the enemy. Healing begins when we combat these distortions about the character of God and begin addressing the wounds of our soul.

Thread of Truth for Chapter 2

Bringing our mind, will and emotions under the authority of our spirit is the first step in healing.

Perch and Scour

Father, I thank You for the beautiful gift of salvation. I know there is nothing I can add to the precious gift of Your son's death for my sins. It is my heart's desire to grow in my relationship with You. I acknowledge that often my soul is where I live. My emotions and the thoughts of my mind take control of much of my life. Please help me to begin to discern between my soul and my spirit. Show me Your truths that will bring freedom and healing to my mind, will and emotions. Enlighten the areas where I have used religion to cover pain or ignore areas that You are now ready to bring into Your light and healing.

In humility I lay before You thoughts and beliefs that have held me captive and I ask You to begin the process of bringing them under the authority of Your Spirit.

03

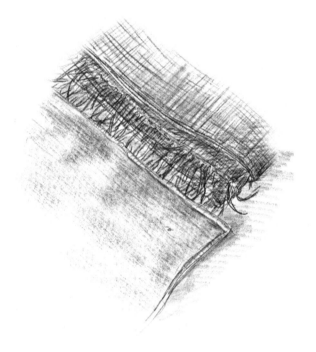

Chapter 03

Frayed at the Ends

Looking For Frayed Ends

No doubt we've all had a favorite sweater, pillow or perhaps wall hanging that with time begins to show wear and the edges fray, or the threads begin to pull out. We may try to snip off the ends or push the vulnerable threads back to the underneath side so that the "look" of the item is preserved, at least for a while. It is no coincidence that a popular saying during times of stress is that one is "frayed around the edges." We can sometimes feel like our edges are loose, and we best tuck them back in before someone notices.

> *We can 'hide' these frayed ends underneath our tapestry, but they don't generally remain hidden for long*

We may feel like the general tapestry is in good shape, but don't look too closely at our item or don't tug on a loose thread or it will all come unraveled.

Much like our reactions to *frayed ends,* we look for ways to conceal trauma rather than allowing the Lord to heal it. This practice is referred to as a ***coping mechanism or a trauma response.*** Some trauma responses are healthy, such as the physical response of adrenaline in the midst of an accident which allows you to lift a car or perform other typically impossible feats. The brain's ability to disassociate in the midst of extreme trauma is actually a protective feature.

However, when these responses are still present after the event has passed, they are often no longer healthy but rather they are inhibitive. If trauma has been a constant in your life, you have likely developed multiple coping mechanisms as a result of it.

Let's first take a look at typical trauma responses. These are often referred to as the **Five F's** - these responses are most common with event centered trauma and are the most likely to have recurring physical manifestations.

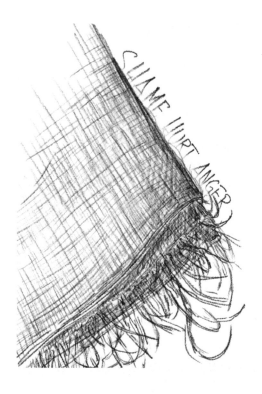

*Like frayed ends, our shame, hurt, anger
and other evidence of trauma creeps
out from under our tapestry and cannot
remain hidden*

The Five F's

Commonly, we hear the term "fight or flight response", but these are just 2 of the five most common responses to a traumatic event.

Fight - physical fighting, struggling, pushing or verbally saying "no."

Flight - creating distance between you and the event, including running or hiding.

Freeze - your body goes tense and still. This is a common response to sexual violence. By freezing, you are not giving consent. This behavior is seen in the animal kingdom where an animal will "play dead" to avoid being seen or eaten by predators.

Flop - this is similar to freezing, except instead of your muscles tensing up, they go limp. This can reduce the physical pain of the event.

Friend - Calling for a friend or bystander or the act of befriending the attacker by negotiating, bribing or pleading with them.

Certainly, there is a great wealth of secular material to read with regard to the effects of trauma. We are purposely giving only a framework of understanding so that we may focus on the healing possibilities. Greater understanding of the intricacies of trauma will not lead to healing. It may lead to a better understanding of how trauma has affected your life and relationships, or it may increase your scientific knowledge with regard to the brain and body's responses, but knowledge alone does not bring healing.

Memory and Triggers

Our memories are very fickle. This is one reason that "eyewitness" accounts are not very dependable. Often in a situation that poses danger, the memory is created based on what we FEEL or PERCEIVE, not necessarily on what is actually happening. Then, when we find ourselves in a situation where there is a similarity to the first event, such as a familiar setting or people group, we react based on a former memory.

Think about this:

Thoughts ⇨ Beliefs ⇨ Emotions ⇨ Choices ⇨ Actions ⇨ Reality

If we don't control what we allow to hang out in our subconscious, we can inadvertently create a course for our lives that is detrimental. When we begin to apply the truth of God's Word to our INNER MAN, we can change the subconscious thought process. There has been a lot of research around the concept of neuroplasticity in the past several years. To reduce this great research to just a few sentences does not give it due justice, for the findings are amazing, both scientifically as well as biblically. This is often referred to as "rewiring your brain."

In the most simplistic definition, neuroplasticity is the brain's ability to morph both physically and functionally due to your environment, thinking and emotions. What we think actually changes the terrain of our brains. With the increased ability for magnetic resonance imaging, we can now even see these changes.

For example, they can now compare the brain scans of two adolescent children and see if there has been ongoing trauma or neglect because it changes the physical brain! When we renew our minds, the body is also renewed. This knowledge is having an incredible impact in the fields of traumatic brain injury recovery, cognitive therapy, learning disabilities, depression and many more.

It's Okay To FEEL

Emotions can at times be **uncontrollable,** however that does not mean they are **unmanageable.** For the most part, our emotions occur spontaneously without our direct permission. We feel joy at the sight of a family member we haven't seen for a long time. We weep at a sad movie or tender moment. Jesus had emotions. He felt joy, anger, sorrow, compassion, and anxiety. The difference is in the fruit of what was produced by His emotions. He did not stuff or "control" His emotions, but rather He brought them under the authority of the Holy Spirit.

In the gospels, Jesus expressed great anxiety about the coming crucifixion. He wrestled with the emotions that were overwhelming and prayed, "Not my will, but Yours be done". (Luke 22:42) In the midst of seeing the hypocrisy of the Pharisees, He became angry and spoke correction, (Matthew 23:33), He felt joy knowing He had pleased the Father, (John 15:10-11). God has given us emotions to experience life and its fullness, but He also gave us a free will and we can use those emotions for delight and fulfillment or for pain and destruction when we allow them to rule over us.

The truth is our emotions are not a true measure of reality

The truth is our emotions are not a true measure of reality. They can be fickle, unreliable and often based in lies. One of the biggest mistakes we make as young believers is to embrace the idea that because I "feel" it, it must be true. We can do this even with the presence of God. Tears shed during worship or prayer do not validate God's presence. They may help us "feel" more connected; however the truth is that God is always with us.

If we rely on a feeling to trust that He is there, we will be tossed about with the winds of circumstance. Jesus left us the Holy Spirit, the Comforter, as the promise of His abiding presence. John 14:26-27 states, "But the Adovcate, the Holy Spirit, whom the Father will send in my name, will teach you all things and will remind you of everything I have said to you. Peace I leave with you. My peace I give to you, not as the world gives. Do not let your hearts be troubled and do not be afraid".

Through prayer, we can often ask the Holy Spirit to come into the place where this memory resides, be it physical or emotional, and release healing into that moment. This is much more effective as we learn to unravel the lies that are typically present as well. We are laying the groundwork in this chapter to address those lies. Don't get frustrated that you aren't seeing immediate healing. These responses and coping mechanisms are interwoven and are often connected to a framework that needs healing as well.

A general prayer of healing over one of these physical responses would look like this:

Father, I come to you and ask that you would meet me with the presence of your Holy Spirit at the moment of the (event). I know that You were with me and You see the way in which my body and soul responded. Would You release my body from the effects of being touched, hit or abused. Would You bring healing to my muscles and my physical body that respond when I am afraid or reminded of the event. Holy Spirit, cover me in Your peace in my mind and body. I bring my body into submission under my spirit and command the physical manifestations to stop in the name of Jesus.

Father, reveal to me any lies that may be surrounding my body's physical responses.

This chapter is meant to uncover, reveal and expose some of the false patterns that we default to when we are stuck in a **trauma response.** You may not be able to determine at this point what responses are based in trauma. To begin to discern these areas - make a list this week of any recurring troubling thoughts.

See if there are any patterns to the areas that are occupying the bulk of your thoughts.

In conjunction with this, hold yourself accountable to journal any moments during the week when you exhibit extreme emotion. This can be elation, fear or anger- literally any emotion you feel that is intense. Also list any moments when you feel devoid of emotion or connection. If you struggle with the self-awareness to do this, ask a trusted friend to help you.

The most common coping mechanisms are:

01   Denial

02   Emotional Response

03   Numbing

04   Running

During a traumatic event our brain will stop or slow down some of its normal functions in order to survive the current threat of the situation. Often when this happens, our brains don't process the trauma correctly. We may have hyper details about some things, and completely misperceive or blank out on other key happenings. Then, out of nowhere, that sound, smell, or fragmented memory comes rushing back, sending our body into a trauma response. This is not a fun way to live, so in an effort to cope, we create coping mechanisms, or the default reactions listed above.

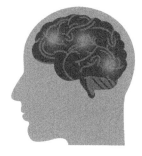

Trauma negatively affects the brain and can spread to other areas

Much like a physical infection that goes untreated, trauma left alone typically spreads to other areas. It isn't really hidden or stuffed. It is doing its work. It is growing and infiltrating other places in our lives. We can deny it, but the reality is that the longer we wait to process trauma, the more often its effects then seep into nearly every relationship we have. Remember trauma can distort our view of God, ourselves and others.

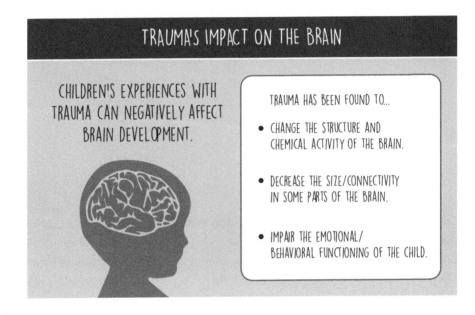

Denial - Not just a River in Egypt

So why do we deny? There can be many reasons. Sometimes the pain of this reality is so deep that it simply doesn't line up with the view we had hoped for in our lives. This incongruity can make us rationalize by saying, "It really wasn't that bad." "My dad wasn't *ALWAYS* drunk." Or it can be the opposite: we know how deep the chasm of pain is and we are overwhelmed.

The thought of opening the door to the hidden things of the past conjures up a fear that can be paralyzing. This is a major lie of the enemy to keep people from pursuing the healing that God so lavishly wants to pour out. It is not the heart of the Father to pull strings out of your tapestry and leave the hole. He is a God of redemption. If He has his finger on an area of your life where He wants to remove a thread, or add in a different color, or tie something off, **His purpose is to restore the Tapestry to its original design.** Remember that He knit us together in our mother's womb.

There is a tapestry that contains your unique spiritual DNA. It is written about you in the spirit. This fallen world and the works of the enemy may distort your picture, but God's heart is always about restoration.

So how do we feel with the anxiety and dread that can arise when we begin to open a past wound? Just as we mentioned in Chapter One, we begin by placing our emotions, our mind and our will under the authority of our spirit. If the enemy has access to your body, he will affect you with shallow breathing, tension headaches or even nausea to keep you from pursuing an area of trauma. You may fear the depth of emotion that has been bottled up for years or worse yet, what if it's so buried that I actually can't feel anything any longer?

Our will comes into play in the realm of denial. We can choose with our will to refuse to pursue our healing. Often our will and denial go hand in hand to make an impenetrable fortress. If you struggle to "feel" memories or emotions because you've denied and stuffed them for the majority of your life, it is good practice to repent for making choices with your will that have inhibited your ability to be honest about your pain. We will deal more with this in the chapter on inner vows and agreements.

What does denial look like in your life?

01   The refusal or avoidance of talking about certain time periods in your life

02   Dissociation

03   Creating an unattainable fantasy life

04   Unresolved grief

What other ways do you see denial affecting your life? Has anyone ever mentioned to you that you were in denial about something? How did this make you feel?

Emotional Response

"Weeping may stay for the night, but rejoicing comes in the morning" Psalm 30:5

Sometimes we need to cry. We need to look trauma square in the face and grieve it or experience the emotions that have been bundled away. Those emotions can be intense. However, when we begin to unpack them at the root level, they cease to have the power to infiltrate all the other areas of our life. The work can be hard, but it is so worth it.

When we begin to address the emotion related to trauma it can at first seem overwhelming. You may want to make sure that you have an adequate support system in place if you are addressing complex trauma or consider having a counselor or ministry team to help you navigate these areas.

As we will unpack in this next section, emotions are not bad. Uncontrolled emotions may give way to sin, but emotions, even the difficult ones, are not wrong. Rage, manic behavior, anxiety and fear can all be directly related to trauma. Often unregulated emotional distress presents as anxiety or depression, two of the most common diagnoses.

When trauma goes unaddressed, it festers and looks for a way to manifest itself. This can be through a panic attack, prolonged depression or a rage-filled outburst. Typically, the longer we allow trauma to go unaddressed, the more symptoms we will begin to see creeping their way to the surface. Those frayed ends don't stay on the underneath side, despite our efforts to conceal them.

Numbing

The correlations between addiction and trauma are endless. Alcohol, drugs, shopping, sex, porn and gambling all serve to numb pain. Of course, they typically end up resulting in secondary wounding or trauma. The longer we numb our pain, the more likely we are to increase the amounts and frequency of our behaviors. While the above numbing tendencies often have a negative impact, we can also choose to numb with exercise, work, social media, or even church.

While these latter things are not bad, they can detour us or become distractions from truly addressing the source of our pain. Many of these activities release dopamine and endorphins, the physiological components that our bodies crave. They may give a momentary escape or distraction, but in and of themselves they do not heal anything.

Numbing can be harder to detect when we aren't abusing drugs, but yet we put in 70 hours at our job. Numbing can be simply the inability to stop and feel. To be present without the need to avoid, hide or busy ourselves is a good indicator that we aren't consumed with numbing our pain.

Avoidance

Lastly, when the numbing wears off, we often will run toward anything that will give a new sense of purpose or hope. We might run from one failed relationship right to another. The new car didn't fill the hole, so we try the new boat. Pilates not exciting anymore? So, we take up weightlifting. There is a constant cycle to fulfill. But you can't fill a bucket that has holes. Stop and take the time to deal with what poked the holes in the first place.

All of these default reactions to trauma are common, so don't beat yourself up if you are realizing you are stuck in one of these phases. Beginning to recognize these phases though, will give you insight into where to begin.

Which of these 4 stages or phases do you see yourself or do you recognise as your behaviors? How long have these behaviors been present? Are you consciously aware that these default mechanisms are an attempt to hide trauma?

Emotions: The Loose Ends

Before we proceed with identifying emotions that we may be experiencing, it is important to establish some foundational truths, so that there are no loose ends. Often when one begins the journey of discipleship and learning to bring the emotions, will and mind under the authority of the spirit, the enemy sets an agenda to distort this biblical principle, causing us to overfocus on intellect, self-protection or self-justification.

Establishing a framework for bringing the mind, will and emotions into submission to the Spirit must embrace the following truths:

01   Emotions are neither bad nor good. Emotions which are not subject to the spirit are most often sinful. Remember, "Be angry and sin not."

02   Trauma is not an excuse to sin. Period. Regardless of your past, you are responsible for your behaviors, attitudes and actions. Do not use the cliché "It's just the way I am."

03   God's presence is not a feeling. Whether we "feel" close to God is not what is true. He is close to you, and longs for you to lean into Him and feel His embrace.

04   Big emotions are met with a BIG GOD.

05   My perceptions or feelings may or may not be true. If they are not yielded to revelation by the Spirit, I risk responding in my flesh.

Research has shown that about 95% of all your emotions and thoughts come from your subconscious mind. Thoughts and emotions are the catalyst for our actions. Have you ever made a decision that was based on emotion, only later to realize you had made a big mistake? Perhaps you believed the false accusation of a loved one and now the relationship is severed. Maybe you quit your job due to a misunderstanding. Drop out of college because you "felt" you couldn't do it? What decisions have you made that were based on feelings that you later regretted?

Threading the Needle

Are you familiar with the biblical story of the rich young ruler? Jesus's response in Matthew 19:24 says that "it is easier for a camel to go through the eye of a needle, than for someone who is rich to enter into the kingdom of God." Wow, that seems a bit harsh, however, God was pointing out that the posture of our heart can literally keep us from moving forward into the manifest kingdom of God. Much like that camel not fitting into the eye of the needle, we can also have some "camels" that restrict God's ability to weave new threads in areas where darkened or distorted cords may have stained or perverted our tapestry. But wait, He's God. Why doesn't He just heal us automatically?

The Master Weaver created us with free will. We always have a choice to respond, to run, to resist or to reveal. Humility and vulnerability must be the first threads that are placed in the needle. Pride says, "I'm okay. I can do it on my own." Pride may show up in the inability to receive godly counsel without excuse or defense. It rears its head when we keep our walls up so high, that no one can penetrate them.

We can hide behind walls, trying to protect ourselves from further hurt

On the other hand, vulnerability says, "I need you God to fill in the tattered and stained areas. I will accept the help of others to keep me securely attached to the loom."

I Peter 5:5b-7 tells us that "God opposes the proud but shows favor to the humble. Therefore, submit yourselves to God. Resist the devil, and he will flee from you. Come near to God and he will come near to you. Wash your hands, you sinners , and purify your hearts, you double minded."

Do you realize you can take this entire course, sit amidst others who receive healing and walk away with absolutely no change, other than perhaps some head knowledge? Take a look at your camels. Purpose your heart's intention to be vulnerable and humble. Sitting in a room of people discussing their hurts honestly and openly can be frightening. But going through life concealing those hurts only leads to isolation.

Perch and Scour

Father, I come to You knowing that there are areas of pride in my heart that keep me from allowing You and others to love me the way I was created to be loved. I confess pride as sin and self-protection. I confess that pride makes me feel stronger than I really am. I choose to take off that mask so that You can heal what lies beneath.

I place myself in Your arms, knowing You are there to protect me. I do not have to protect myself and I do not have to be strong and independent. I confess my tendency to place walls of protection around myself. Help me to find a safe community where those walls of independence can safely come down. I choose to embrace You, Jesus, as my Healer and I humbly confess my need for You as Savior and the body of Christ to help guide me and show me truth about You, my past and my future.

Jesus, show me the ways and patterns that I use to avoid dealing with pain and hurt in my past. I no longer want to numb, deny or avoid. I choose to feel what may be unpleasant, knowing that you will not leave me in that emotion, but lead me to healing.

04

Chapter 04

Identity - The Artist's Initials

It is the customary tradition of weavers to leave their initials woven into the lower right-hand corner of a garment or tapestry. They are marking and claiming the work as their own. Sometimes the initials are prominent and sometimes they are purposely hidden or concealed. God too, as the Master Artist, places His initials on us. He marks us as His own.

Our Master Artist has labeled us as His own

The artwork is more and more identifiable as we yield to His craftsmanship and weaving. Identity is woven into the creation by the artist. In many famous tapestries of the Renaissance, the weaver would place the story the tapestry was to tell on a piece of linen sewn in at the bottom. Other prominent artists such as Raphael, created a border compartment to mark his work such as *'Acts of the Apostles.'* Within the border, the mark of the workshop responsible for weaving was prominent, as well as a coat of arms, typically depicting the owner of the tapestry.

Borders ranged from the simple to the extravagant and often distinguished one artist from another. Make no mistake that we as believers are to be distinguished from the lives around us. Our lives are hemmed in by the border of the Master Artist. We are to be defined by Him as He leaves His mark indelibly upon us.

The enemy uses events and situations throughout our lives to attack the fiber of our identity and our relationship with God. If he is able to establish lies about our identity, value and worth at a very young age, we grow up believing these fallacies, often not even recognizing them as lies. He attempts to thwart the original design and defame and mark the canvas with destruction, self-doubt, worthlessness and isolation from God and others. He cleverly does this by deceiving us into thinking that the lies we listen to from childhood are not only true, but also that they originate from us, instead of from the pit of hell.

The voice that we internalize in our early youth is typically the voice we tend to identify with the strongest. It is the most "known." We have a hard time determining that it isn't, "just the way I am," but a systematic weaving of untruths, misunderstandings and in some cases sin responses, that keep us attached to this voice. If that voice is self-critical or self-loathing due to years of judgment and the need to "earn" love, we are not in a good place to accurately evaluate our worth. Our view of self can be extremely untrustworthy and unreliable. We may have a distorted sense of importance, resulting in arrogance and self-centeredness or we may instead view ourselves as the lowliest of worms. Relying on our own voice to tell us who we are is not where we want to plant the measuring stick.

Learning to look to the One who created us for the definition of our worth is the beginning of establishing a firm foundation. When we buy a TV, coffee maker or drone, we don't look online for the owner's manual of a bicycle to build or repair what we've purchased. Sounds silly, but it's true, so why would we look anywhere other than the true Owner's manual of scripture to determine how and why we were created?

01   We were created by a Creator.

02   Our spirits were bought with a price of sacrifice, by Christ's atonement on the cross. We have great worth.

03   We have a purpose and destiny given to us by God and God alone.

This type of study leads to some of the most existential and philosophical treatises of all time. Books abound on "finding yourself" or increasing your potential. Man from the beginning of time has asked, "What is the meaning of life?" Let's settle that one big question right here: **To know God and to enjoy Him forever, is our ultimate purpose.**

Have you met people who are just so secure in the Father's love for them that it oozes out of them? It can even be unsettling to those of us who struggle with our own worth. We have included several scriptures which speak of God's love and care toward us, but the truth is until we move away the blockages that don't line up with these truths it can seem as if we are simply reciting a narrative meant for someone else. We may even believe theologically that these things are true, but if they are not true in our SPIRIT, we will not experience the joy and freedom that knowing our worth and identity can bring.

Certainly, as scripture says, we can renew our mind. Dwelling on scripture is a great way to begin that renewal process, but if after memorizing and praying these scriptures you are not finding any sense of breakthrough, you may want to seek ministry to determine what the blockages are if they are not already evident through some of our work thus far.

You know when I sit and when I rise; you perceive my thoughts from afar, Psalm 139:2

God determined the exact time of your birth and where you would live, Acts 17:26

My plan for you is a future and a hope, Jeremiah 29:11

You are my treasured possession, Exodus 19:5

Before you were in your mothers' womb, I knew you, Jeremiah 1:4-5

You were made in my image, Genesis 1:27

I gave up everything that I might gain your love, Romans 8:31-32

Nothing will ever separate you from the love that is in Christ Jesus, Romans 8:38-39

It may sound trite, but until we truly understand the love of the Father and the value and worth He ascribes to us, we will constantly doubt our worth and purpose. We will spend the remainder of this course removing lies that distort that truth. Please know that the steps we outline are for a framework only. You must always rely on the voice of the Holy Spirit. No teaching or prayer method will ever adequately touch you the way one moment with the Holy Spirit can do. However, knowing some basic principles of how to address wounding, lies and the role of the demonic gives you an arsenal of tools to refer to when you are walking through your journey.

Who Do You Say I Am?

Throughout scripture another important pattern we see is that of God's repeated question, "Who do you say that I am?" He asks this question throughout both the Old and New Testament. He desires our response. Moses first asked this question in Exodus. He knew God had sent him to the Israelites, but he also knew he had no relationship or authority with them. Moses was raised in the palaces of the Pharoah. He knew he could not go to the children of Israel in his own name. He asked God, "What am I to tell them when they ask who has sent me?" His reply, "Tell them I AM has sent me to you."

Throughout the Old Testament, He answers, "I Am that I Am." He was to be known by His character, by His attributes. There were many gods in that time, but He was I AM that I AM – no beginning, no end, not made in the image of anything or anyone else. In the New Testament Jesus asks his disciples, "Who do you say that I am?"

In Matthew 16, Peter replies to the question posed by Jesus, "You are the Messiah, the Son of the Living God." Jesus replies, "Blessed are you, Simon son of Jonah, for this was not revealed to you by flesh and blood, but by my Father in heaven."

We began this journey by defining the character and nature of God. As we continue, it is now time to define who we are.

Let's start at the beginning with Adam and Eve. As soon as sin entered, they began the process of being separated from God. They, like us, were created for relationship. When they partnered with sin, the result was a loss of IDENTITY AND RELATIONSHIP, two key components for healing. They doubted their relationship with God and felt rejected. They then experienced shame and fear, two emotions that were previously foreign to them.

We, like Adam and Eve, attempt to deal with our pain and sin by covering and hiding. Fig leaves don't remove shame any better than our coping mechanisms. These faulty ways of dealing with pain caused Adam and Eve to run from God instead of to Him. The enemy's game plan has not changed - his goal is to break relationship between you and the Father. He does this by attacking and accusing your identity, purpose and relationships with God, self and others.

Identity Is Formed....Names Are Given

All throughout scriptures God uses names to define, reform and and establish persons, nations and destinies. Often a person's name was changed based upon the work of God in their life, such as the case for Peter, Sarah and Jacob. Just as these names define or explain the character of a person, God wanted us to know His name, the attributes of His character. "Who do you say that I am?" is a powerful statement. Our answer as we've previously discussed can determine how we relate to God, especially in times of trouble.

But what about our names, our identity? How are they formed? God says, "Before you were in the womb, I knew you." Our lives and identities are sometimes a far cry from what God would have destined for us. This can be the result of our family of origin, place of birth, sin committed against us or even the result of our own choices. These unique situations and our responses to them begin to bring color to our tapestries as our God-given personality emerges more and more or they can instead erode the brilliance of the colors God intended us to have when He knit us together in the womb. At times, things that God intended to be an incredible blessing to us such as our family, can actually be the place where the colors in our tapestry begin to fade or disappear altogether. Every experience and subsequent reaction has the ability to bring truth or wrap us in a lie and distort our colors.

This process of adding color to yarn is called acid washing. Wool yarn that is placed on the skein is typically raw and unbleached. This is like us at birth — essentially a blank canvas, waiting to be filled with beautiful color. The wool yarn goes through a process of scouring to wash and prepare it to receive dye. These dyes are highly concentrated powders which permeate all the fibers. Perhaps that beautiful musical gift you have is a deep rich purple or your ability to grasp mathematical concepts easily is a bright yellow. The uncanny ability to see and feel the needs of others is a warm orange. These beautiful hues, when added, start out rich and untarnished. But in the wrong environment these colors may become bleached and bland.

Just as acid dye brings color to the tapestry, so God has an array of unique colors He has made for us to have in our being, making up our individual identity. Are your colors strong and vibrant or have they faded or disappeared altogether? Do you even know what colors were placed in your original design?

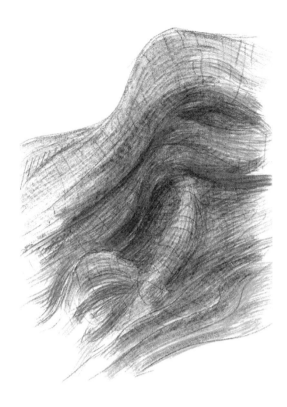

Our Master Weaver has designed us to be full of different hues

How and where does it happen? Is it a choice, an event, a series of events? Does it happen slowly or quickly? Determining where we lost our God given identity can be easy for some to identify and for others, much more challenging. If these exercises are not as valuable for you, it may be that your trauma is not as wrapped as intrinsically with your identity as it is for others. Regardless, walking through these steps will help you to add more comprehensive information to your trauma timelines as we develop them.

Begin with these simple questions about your early childhood:

    :: Did I feel accepted and valued?

    :: Was I encouraged or berated?

Our brains develop in stages, both in utero as well as in our childhood. When significant trauma occurs during these crucial years, the effect can have a much greater impact with issues such as bonding and identity. Trauma in early childhood can result in hyper arousal of the stress hormones which leads to chronic sensitivity to stress. There are two main types of early trauma which are pervasive: the child who experiences neglect, and the child who experiences physical threat or harm.

When a child experiences deprivation, they require interventions which require learning and input. A child who has experienced threat requires interventions which target safety and cognitive interventions. Unfortunately, many experience both as well as the direct influences of genetics, mental health and the effects of poor nutrition due to poverty. Children who are exposed early to trauma often struggle with behavioral regulation, executive functioning, sensory stimuli and social information processing.

If you are aware of early neglect or abuse in your story, it is important to minister to these deficits, even if you are not aware of the specific events. Unfortunately, in the realms of both psychotherapy and inner healing there have been methodologies which encourage the use of guided imagery which very frequently creates false memories. If you are aware that neglect or abuse was present, Jesus can heal that without specific knowledge of events.

It is not necessary to dredge up or visualize any aspect of trauma for it to be healed. We can open doors for the enemy to torment when we allow our imagination to create scenarios, rather than dealing with only known incidents or those shown directly to us by the Holy Spirit. If you are not familiar with the voice of the Holy Spirit, caution should be used when trusting visions or memories as the enemy will counterfeit, if this is not an area of strength.

Our identities are not formed by knowledge, they are formed by **experiences.** We shape our beliefs about ourselves through the lens of how others treat us whether it be parents, caregivers or peers. When these interactions are secure and attached, we develop the ability to build relationships and bond, but when these relationships are unreliable or worse even volatile, we stay inward, creating patterns of mistrust and self-language which tells us that we are unworthy of being loved.

When you doubt your own worth and identity, it is not possible to become the creation who God planned for you since the beginning of time. This is the enemy's ultimate end game. He is not attacking the two-year-old, he is seeking to destroy the given destiny, calling and purpose of the adult that the two-year-old will BECOME. The enemy is not creative in his plan, and this is why he so desperately targets the youth through cartoons filled with demonic overtures, hypersexualized school curriculums and movies which portray believers as Bible thumping idiots.

The enemy rules the world and he uses that authority to attack minds and lives before they have the opportunity to move forward in their positioning with Christ. Think about it - if we spend the bulk of our time as believers trying to heal from wounding we received in our early lives, we are detracted from our purpose from serving Christ and building the kingdom.

These voices continue into our adult lives. The opinion and actions of others greatly influence who we believe we are as well as our value. We were created to have close bonds of relationship. Early on these relationships served the purpose of tribal identity and protection, but now we have our own cultural "tribes" which dictate what is and isn't "acceptable." As teens we call it peer pressure, but lest we think we as adults are saved from this type of influence, just take a look at your social media accounts, the brands you buy, the items in your home and the activities you are involved in. Culture can deceptively influence our view of self and how well or not well we "belong." How well do you do at not allowing culture to dictate your sense of belonging?

Childhood trauma can have a devastating effect not only on one's self-worth and attachment, but it typically sets the stage for how we see the world. Wounds of childhood, such as neglect, shame and rejection are substantially more powerful because we lack the necessary skills and resilience to withstand the onslaught. Regardless of how the trauma occurred in childhood or adulthood, it changes your perception of the world. Everyone's responses to trauma are different, but there are definite patterns that are seen. Some of the most common trauma responses are listed below.

:: anxiety

:: chronic anger

:: flashbacks, nightmares or intrusive memories

:: change in appetite

:: shutting down

:: difficulty focusing

:: feeling out of your body or disconnected

:: rigidity or requiring things be done a certain way

:: self harm

:: engaging in risky or dangerous behaviors

:: avoidance of relationships or activities that once brought joy

:: use of alcohol or drugs to numb anxiety or pain

:: feeling unsafe

Each of these manifestations can wreak havoc on our relationships and are often the blame for the chaos and turmoil that is misplaced at the feet of a spouse, job, child or friend. We learn through childhood how to attach to parents, family members, and caregivers. These attachment styles often follow us well into adulthood. When our present attachments are secure, we most likely had supportive childhood caregivers. Chaos, dysfunction, generational trauma and neglect are pivotal factors affecting how we learn to relate with the world around us.

Wait, who's talking?

Sometimes we are not able to identify where the voice came in that undermined our worth. Often in this case, you may be dealing with a generational curse or thematic lie. A thematic lie is a pervasive series of events or a culture that brings harm to our life. For example, you may have never been hit by your father, so there were no physical bruises, yet his constant raging and abuse of your mother, caused you to believe no man is to be trusted and you still cower when you feel tension in a room.

Another example would be that despite having adequate jobs, your family struggled to meet basic needs such as adequate food and housing. You were never told you weren't good enough, but intrinsically you knew you were somehow "less than others." You felt it in the stares of your peers, the whispers of your distant family members. These lies can be powerful as they are woven into the fabric of our lives. Sometimes they are so subtle, we actually believe that the voice we hear is us, when all along it is the voice of the enemy or the voice of our past whispering those nasty lies into our head.

A thematic lie is often one of the most difficult types of memories or lies to minister to because it is not based on a specific event or events. It is most likely the result of the ABSENCE of good rather than the prevalence of bad. If we were not nurtured or our personal identity not supported, it is far harder to define than being hit or abused. Identifying one root cause of a thematic lie may be difficult, but yet it must still be addressed and brought to truth.

Look at the following statements and check the ones you believe are true. You may rationally know they aren't true, but yet you believe them.

- [ ] My birth was an accident or I am unwanted
- [ ] I have committed sins that are not forgivable
- [ ] I am unworthy of love
- [ ] God is angry with me
- [ ] God is distant
- [ ] God abandoned me when I was hurt
- [ ] I am defective or broken
- [ ] I have no future
- [ ] My value is less than others
- [ ] I am rejected
- [ ] I am alone
- [ ] I am stupid
- [ ] I am dirty
- [ ] I deserve to be hurt

Generational Curses and Blessings

Scripture says that the sins of the fathers are passed down to the fourth generation. This can be a difficult concept to grasp, so if this brings confusion, please read this section multiple times to understand the entirety of the concept. First of all, make NO mistake, YOU ARE NOT RESPONSIBLE FOR THE SINS OF YOUR ANCESTORS. That is a Biblical principle. However, we can be affected by the sins of our parents, grandparents etc, going back to the 4th generation, because that is also scriptural.

This means that there can be sins which are committed by those before us that have an effect upon us. That sounds unfair doesn't it? When we look at the aspect of the blood in scripture, that is where life is contained. It is why Jesus had to shed His blood for the forgiveness of our sins. Nothing else would have saved us but by the shedding of His innocent blood as the Lamb of God. Both blessing and cursing are passed down generationally.

When we serve God and make righteous choices, we are passing down spiritual blessing to our children, and conversely when sins are committed, especially those which include blasphemy, sexual sin, murder, addictions and such, those propensities are passed down. Does this mean you are responsible for this sin? NO, but what it does mean is that you may be struggling with something more strongly because of the sins of your ancestors. Certainly, some of this can also be magnified by environmental factors. There is now also evidence that trauma can change the DNA of a person. So, when a family has a series of traumatic events, their DNA is actually changed and flows from generation to generation. Learning to break off generational sins can bring immediate freedom to many people and should be a regular practice of personal ministry. Sometimes the effect is grandiose, other times it is minimal, but it is always a good practice to call forward the generational blessings and remove the generational curses.

Let's start with the blessings. Perhaps you don't know what your generational blessings are, or perhaps you do not come from a lineage of Christians. If not, let the blessings start with you now.

Example Prayer

Know therefore that the Lord your God is God: he is the faithful God, keeping his covenant of love to a thousand generations of those who love him and keep his commandments. (Deut 7:9-11, Ps 103:17-18)

No weapon forged against you will prevail, and you will refute every tongue that accuses you. This is the heritage of the servants of the Lord, and this is their vindication from me, declares the Lord.(Is 54:17)

A good person leaves an inheritance for their children's children, but a sinner's wealth is stored up for the righteous (Prov 13:22)

The Spirit you received does not make you slaves, so that you live in fear again; rather, the Spirit you received brought about your adoption to sonship, and by him we cry, "Abba Father" (Roman 8:15)

The righteous lead blameless lives; blessed are their children after them. (Prov 20:7)

What would be an example of a generational blessing?

01   Obedience to God

02   Joy

03   Strong, faithful marriages

04   Fertility

Just as God gave each of the 12 tribes special gifts and positions around the tabernacle in the wilderness, He gives families, nations and tribes certain attributes which are defining for them. They are part of His plan and purpose. If you've never thought about this before, begin to ask God what are the callings and purposes over my life? Where am I to live? What am I supposed to do as a career? But more specifically for this chapter, God, what are the generational blessings over my family line?

Biblical Causes for Curses

A curse is the direct result of disobedience by self or family line. Biblically we see examples of pestilence, madness, blindness and sickness as examples (Deut 28 and Deut 28:15).

To address the idea of curses, we must define what we are really talking about. Often when we think of the word "curse", we conjure up the picture of a woman with a black coned hat mixing eye of newt and various herbs and spouting incantations. Absolutely, if there is occult involvement in our generational line then we want to address those situations, but often these curses are not quite so blatant. They are more than just assumed behaviors. They often involve the shedding of blood, violence or sexual perversion. All of these types of sin affect the bloodline. This is not to say that other sins do not, it is just that these specific types of sins most often have generational effects.

It is not required to go looking for all the evil that is in our generational line, but awareness is important. If you are plagued with particular strongholds that you just can't seem to get free from, ask the Lord to show you if there are any generational ties or sins that need to be broken. Again, you are not repenting for the sin on your own behalf, but for the bloodline. You are commanding that connection to be broken off and no longer hinder. You are asking God to cleanse and restore.

Word Curses

The power of life and death is in the tongue. Words have power.

01   You were never wanted.

02   You are the black sheep

03   You're stupid

04   It's your fault

So many phrases that ring in our ears are the results of word curses that have been spoken over us or behind us, both the known and unknown (Prov 18:31, Isaiah 65, James 3:9- 11, Prov 11:9).

Sin Curses

Abraham lied, Jacob lied (Gen 20:2, 27:7).

Eve's sin led to pain in childbirth(Gen 3:16).

Generational curses affect a nation(Is 24).

Curses can affect increase "You sow a wind and reap a whirlwind" (Hosea 8:7).

Children suffer from the sins of their fathers (II Sam 12:1-19.)

Also see: Deut 5:9 23:2,3 38:45,46, 58,59; Num 14:18; Lev 26:40-42; Ex 25:3,4 34:67; Isaiah 65:6,7; Dan 9:16; Matt 2:7:25; John 9:1-2

We've discussed how the words and actions of others shape our identity. But now, we need to take a look at how a broken identity can shape our behaviors and lives. When we are wounded, it affects our choices and therefore our destinies. Have you ever not done something for fear that you would fail? Ever avoid a party or event because you didn't feel like you "fit in?"

A difficult subject to broach is the aspect of a victim mentality. No one ever wants to cast blame at the feet of someone who has been traumatized. Blame is not the intention of this section, but rather to illuminate another subtle trick of the enemy. If over time we begin to agree with the lies of the enemy to the point that those lies become our identity or our defense, it can become a great hindrance to healing. Even in the most horrific of events, God gives us a CHOICE as to how we respond.

This is one of the most difficult things to comprehend in the midst of ministering to someone who has been raped, wounded or abused. It also explains the phenomenon that occurs when someone is wounded and the vast difference in how people respond. Let's look at a simple example. Two women are brutally raped as young women. Woman one builds a fortress of self-protection and shuts relationships out and begins a motto of "I can conquer the world in my own strength." Woman two becomes a recluse, rarely leaving her apartment. She avoids relationships and all change. These are two overly simplistic scenarios, but the point is HOW we respond to the lie of trauma can have a profound impact on how we move forward. If the enemy can make us feel helpless and that we are ALWAYS the one who is wounded, wronged, or marginalized, we can pick up a spirit of victimization which will hinder the work of God in our lives.

The lie of victimization can hinder a person from activating their own will. It is what causes people to stop fighting altogether, to accept whatever abuse is levied at them. It can also, with time, convince a person that they do not have choices, they do not have authority and autonomy and a valid voice. When victimization becomes sin, it is used as a weapon to defend behaviors and excuse responsibilities for choices we make. One does not abuse their children because they were abused. It is a choice we make. There can be habits and response patterns that we've learned, but our past NEVER allows us to excuse our own sin.

A spirit of victimization is often easy to see for those who have keen discernment. Some people wear the scars of their trauma both in their physical body and in their souls. This marking often draws further abuse to them and continues the lie, through no fault of the victim. It is just a tactic of the enemy. An example of this is a child who is molested or traumatized at a young age. Often due to their abuse, they do not develop healthy physical boundaries and can be drawn to befriending unsafe and preying people. Abusers look for children who are quiet, set apart from the group or looking for attention, as easy prey.

Breaking the mindset of victimization begins with recognizing the lies imposed by the abuse. It is often also helpful to work with a therapist to strengthen and engage the person's will. Our will is part of our soul as we discussed in Chapter One. Our will is the place of our inner strength. It must be engaged and aligned with the purposes and plan of Christ. We can and do do things in our own strength, but that power is magnified when we submit our will to the strength of the Father.

Many times, we will begin prayers with, "As an act of my will." Sometimes emotionally or with our intellect we are not ready to engage the promises or the actions of obedience, such as forgiveness. Engaging the will into agreement with what our spirit wants is part of bringing the body, soul (mind, will and emotions) UNDER the authority of our spirit.

Proverbs 18:21 says that, "The tongue has the power of life and death, and those who love it will eat its fruit." Wow that is powerful....we have the ability to CHOOSE.

Perch and Scour

Jesus I long to see the vibrant colors that You placed within me. I desire to know my name and the purposes written over me in the spirit. Begin with my earliest experiences of bonding and security, help me to see where there are blessings and help me to see where there was lack. I want my identity to be built on what You placed inside me. Please show me the events that shape my views negatively about myself, God and others.

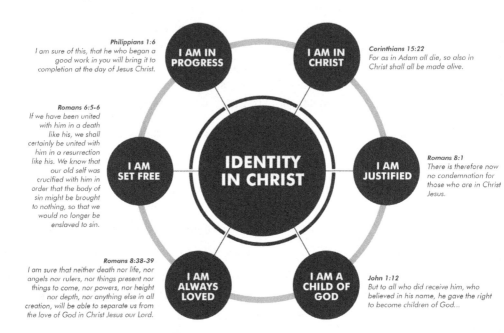

Lord, I know that there are blessings in my bloodline, and I thank You for them. I take this time to ask You to release the fullness of the generational blessings in my family line. I come into agreement with any spiritual promises or callings that have been lost or abandoned. Father, I ask that any curses that may be in my family line be severed and removed. I bring the events and curses that I am aware of to You and ask that You place them under the blood of your Son. I come out of agreement with any sin committed or ideology embraced that is not of You. Release my life from the effects of these sins and curses. Father, I specifically bring to You any curses that would keep me from feeling the depths of Your love or seeing the purposes and plans for my life.

As an act of my will, I come out of agreement with all beliefs, attitudes and spirits of victimization. Remove from me any effects of abuse and wounding that would draw like experiences or spirits to me. I choose to partner with the truth and promises that are written over me in the spirit.

05

Chapter 05

Unraveling the Lies

When we look at the backside of a tapestry, we often see the knotted, frayed and distorted image. This is where lies often lay - dormant and subtle, attaching to our identity, our memories and often our futures. When these lies are not dealt with, they often bleed into the visible part of the tapestry, blatantly obvious for those around us to identify. When we partner with a lie long enough it has the power to shape our identity instead of being shaped by the image of God.

In the weaver's toolbox there is a tool called a *'sleying hook.''* This small flat tool is used to pull the end threads of the warp through the comb-like reed. The reed separates and spaces the warp threads. The sleyhook, which by the way, is such a great name, gives us a perfect picture of taking out a wayward thread or calling things into alignment. This very practice of taking a lie captive is second only to the power found in the blood and authority of Christ for tearing down the plans and schemes of the enemy.

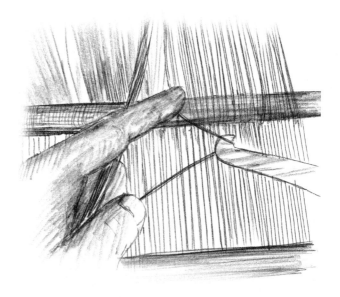

The sleyhook is used here to pull out a wayward thread and bring things back into alignment

At the root of most trauma is an agreement with a lie. This holds true with nearly every trauma type, with the exception of some event-based trauma. Some of these lies are about God, some about us and at times a lie is about another person or situation. We will spend many chapters discussing how to unravel or pull out these lies. For now, let's establish HOW a lie enters. We call these **OPEN DOORS.** The enemy is a legalist and he will use any of the following ways to embed into you a lie about you, God or others.

01   Personal sin

02   Sin committed against you

03   Generational sin

04   An event such as a car wreck, accident or natural disaster

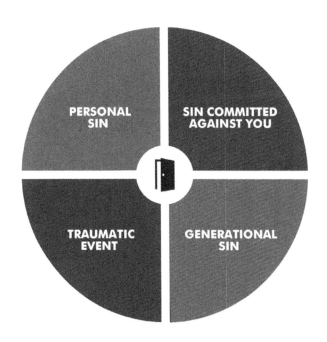

These lies, left unchecked, become embedded in the mind, will, emotions and body of the person causing a **STRONG HOLD.** These lies can come through singular events or the culmination of perpetual messages and lies that we pick up through our experiences.

If you are a female, you have undoubtedly had the following experience (guys, please indulge us for a moment). You open your jewelry box to find that one of your favorite necklaces has become tangled...massively tangled. You work and work to move the chain in just the right manner to loosen the knot. If you pull on the wrong part of the knot, you actually tighten the grip of the entanglement. It can be a painstaking process leading to frustration and sometimes a trip to the jewelry store for just the right tools to untangle the fragile, yet important belonging.

We are much like those delicate chains. We sometimes get knotted up. Whether it is a ball of string or a jewelry chain, pulling on any random thread can actually strengthen the hold of the knot. Understanding how to apply the truth of God's Word to each individual thread to loosen its grip is key to unraveling the lies or knots the enemy has created.

Let's start with unraveling lies that surround events. One important thing to remember is that our **perception** of an event may have interpreted trauma, even when it was not present. This most often occurs in parent - child relationships. A child's immature social awareness or ability to perceive abstract concepts can lead them to interpret and receive trauma, even when it was not present.

Event Based Traumas

Events such as wrecks, natural disasters or physical violence most often leave lies such as:

I am not safe

I am alone

I am a victim

I am weak

God did not protect me from.....

Physical acts of trauma can leave obvious scars and manifestations on our bodily responses such as panic attacks, emotional paralysis, the inability to drive, or be alone for example. The open door is the event itself. The enemy enters through at the point of the trauma to establish a lie.

Many times, a simple healing prayer of closing the open door at the point of the incident is enough to stop panic attacks and physical manifestations such as flashbacks and nightmares.

A sample prayer for an event such as this could be:

Father, we ask in your name that you touch my mind, body and emotions at the point of entry from my (name the incident). I ask that You remove any spirits of fear, anxiety or abandonment that entered at that point. Father, bring Your healing to every part of my mind, body and emotions that were affected by this event. Please reveal any lies that I now believe as a result of this incident. I come out of agreement that I am alone, abandoned or a victim. You are my Shield, my Healer and my Protector.

When the event involves sin done against you such as a violent or sexual act, it is important to acknowledge forgiveness. If this does not come readily, at this point, that's okay. We will deal with this more later.

Personal Sin

God, the ultimate "good parent" sets boundaries for his children to keep them safe. When we wander outside those boundaries, we open doors to the effects and LIES of the enemy. Sin is an open door. We may at times be able to sin for a period of time without seeing immediate results in our lives. At other times, a personal sin has immediate and far-reaching consequences, but sin ALWAYS opens a door.

If you are from the Midwest or the South, you have undoubtedly heard the phrase, "Shut the door, were you raised in a barn?" The obvious connotation is that barns allow animals to wander in and out, but houses are to have doors which keep the "critters" out. This is the same with our personal lives. Keeping the doors closed keeps the critters out.

Personal holiness is one of the strongest defenses against ongoing attack and infestation of the enemy. An issue that comes up frequently in the areas of inner healing and deliverance is that the person often wants to feel better but does not want to shut the doors. This lack of personal responsibility and personal conviction can lead to the issues actually becoming worse. If there is not repentance in an area, there cannot be freedom. That is a spiritual principle that God does not violate.

We can open doors to the enemy before we realize we have even sinned, or through sins committed before we were believers. The issue is not one of condemnation, but of restoration of the territory where the enemy had gained access. When we confess a sin, that territory now belongs to Jesus. The blood of Jesus is literally what says to the enemy, "You may NOT cross this line." Often the sin we committed may not be the actual lie that is causing trauma, it can be any type of accompanying lie that the enemy attacks us with as a result of our sin. His favorites are guilt, shame and condemnation, just to name a few. We will deal with these familiar foes in a different chapter. For now, we are focusing on the sin acts themselves.

It can be difficult at times to look at our sin head-on without engaging with the shame, regret or grief that accompanies them. The first step is getting honest about our sin, without justification and rationalization, to begin the healing process. If your heart has hardened or feels calloused about a certain issue, you may want to spend time asking the Lord to soften your heart and give you a true spirit of repentance. Again, we are looking for spiritual fruit here, not a religious act or belief. Remember, it is God's kindness that leads us to repentance, not his judgment or anger.

Perch and Scour for personal sins

Dear Jesus,

I come to You and ask that You forgive me for _____

_____.

I know that by sinning in this way, I opened a door for the enemy to attack my life with lies. I ask that You cover me with Your grace and mercy and that by Your blood You wash away this sin and all its effects. I ask that You close the doors that were opened by my sin. I ask that You forgive me for any way that this sin harmed others. I know that when I repent, You forgive me completely and I agree to walk now as a person who is forgiven and free.

Sin Done Against Us

This is by far the most common area of trauma because we live in a fallen world. As the saying goes, "Hurt people, hurt people." Much like an improperly cured fabric that bleeds onto everything around it when wet, the sins and actions of others can stain our tapestry. If throughout the bulk of our lives we've been surrounded by others with unhealed trauma, we can likely see the areas in our own lives that have been adversely affected. Remember some sins done against us are those of omission, not just commission. The absent father, the home lacking any physical demonstration of affection, the home lacking protection from drugs and alcohol - all of these scenarios bleed onto the very fibre of our being, tinting and at times distorting the original design.

The actions and sins of others close to us can affect and 'bleed' onto the fabric of our being with the fabric of who they are

Sometimes these incidents are singular in nature, such as a betrayal, molestation, a robbery, being wrongfully terminated or accused and many other examples. Other times, the sin done against is 'thematic' in nature, meaning it is a constant set of circumstances such as neglect, racism, abandonment, rejection, intimidation and so forth that we are subjected to for a significant amount of time, weaving the lies into the very fiber of our identity.

These types of thematic lies are often the most difficult to recognize because we often misinterpret them to be "just the way I am." We take on the identity of the lie, such as shame or rejection as part of our person, not realizing it is based on an ongoing series of events which plants within us lies about ourselves, God or others.

As we learned with personal sin, unraveling the lie always starts with forgiveness. Recognizing the pattern of God, others and self is helpful to assure that we are closing all of the doors that may be open regarding a specific area of trauma. As we will discuss in a separate chapter, forgiving someone for a wrong does not in ANY way condone the action. It simply removes you from the tie to the perpetrator as well as removing yourself as the judge, a position which belongs solely to God.

Truly forgiving another person who has wronged us can take time to process and truly mean it, much like repentance. A prayer we often utilize is the aspect of engaging one's WILL to forgive. You may not feel any emotion attached to forgiveness, particularly at the beginning. Choosing to engage your WILL to forgive, allows the Father to begin the work of releasing your heart, soul and spirit to truly walk in freedom.

Perch and Scour for sins done against you

Father, I bring to You (name the offender). I am choosing as an act of my will to forgive them for (name the act). When this happened, I felt ashamed, angry, abandoned (describe everything that you felt). I ask that You break any unholy soul ties I may have with this person as a result of the sin. Father, I release them to You and I give up my position to hold them in bondage to me by unforgiveness. I ask that I now be released from this offense, and I release them. Father, if there are any open doors that were opened as a result of this sin done to me, please reveal the lies that I believe as a result of this event. I bring each of these lies to You and ask that You bring truth to each of them.

Generational Sin

This is an area that is often not addressed, but yet can have a very strong effect on a person's ability to completely walk in freedom in an area. The most often quoted verse which references this is Exodus 34:7, *Who forgives iniquity, transgression and sin; yet He will by no means leave the guilty unpunished, visiting the iniquity of fathers on the children and the grandchildren to the third and fourth generations.* This is referenced again in Numbers 14:18 and Deuteronomy 5:9. These verses are identical in their reference, while the following are more general in nature: Isaiah 14:21 and Isaiah 65:7.

This is also referenced in Jeremiah 31:29, Jeremiah 32:18 and a New Testament reference in John 9:2, *Rabbi, who sinned, this man or his parents, that he would be born blind?* However, let us be very clear that no man is responsible for the sin of another, but that is different from being affected by it. Ezekiel 18:20 clearly explains this, "The person who sins will die. The son will not bear the punishment for the son's iniquity; the righteousness of the righteous will be upon himself, and the wickedness of the wicked will be upon himself."

When we think of generational sin or even generational curses, we are looking at an open door in the bloodline. As we know, LIFE is in the blood. This is stated in Leviticus 17:14 as well as being listed in Deuteronomy. When we look at when the Israelites entered the Promised Land, which is a metaphor for freedom and or for heaven, we see that God was very purposeful to explain that there would be both BLESSING and CURSING that was released on their bloodlines in accordance with the obedience they had shown.

Deuteronomy 11:26-29 records the Lord's words to Israel: "See, I am setting before you today a blessing and a curse - the blessing if you obey the commands of the Lord your God that I am giving you today; the curse if you disobey the commands of the Lord. When you enter the land you are possessing you are to proclaim on Mt Gerazim the blessings and on Mount Ebal the curses."

Salvation is in the blood of Jesus. The actions of our ancestors can and does affect our ability to see, hear and believe truth. It can set us up for a propensity toward anger, false belief systems, critical thinking, addiction and a vast variety of other sins. Sometimes these open doors lie dormant because we do not engage with them. However, for others the slightest engagement with a sin area that they have a propensity for can become a major obstacle in their spiritual life.

No doubt that some of these areas/ characteristics are also genetic in nature, while some are enhanced by the environment. All of these factors weave together to create a web that often needs untangling. We can repent for the sins of our ancestors. This does not mean that their sins are forgiven because we repent, as is taught in some foreign religions. It simply means that we are separating ourselves from the effects of that sin upon ourselves and our further generational lines.

When you work on your trauma timeline for this chapter, look past the major traumas of mental illness, accidents, suicides etc. Look for thought patterns, behaviors and emotional entanglements which result in a lack of freedom. Also, look at patterns of those who have walked away from Christianity or open doors to the occult etc. This will give you an idea of where you want to focus your prayers. It is also a good practice to pray over your children and break these things off as you are doing this in your own life.

Perch and Scour - Generational sin

Father, I come to You and acknowledge that Your blood breaks the yoke and effects of sin on my bloodline. I repent and separate myself, and my children from the effects of the sin of (name it). I break this curse and sin off my bloodline back to the 4th generation on both my mother and father's side. I ask that You remove all curses, open doors and propensity toward sin in this area. I cover myself with the blood of Jesus and declare that I am free to walk in complete healing and freedom in this area.

Recognizing Open Doors in Our Lives

When we face a difficult situation, we often default to response patterns that can be based in trauma, or what we refer to as trauma triggers. If we only look at the immediate reaction, emotion or situation we will most often miss the true open door. We cast blame at the feet of our children, our stress, our spouse or boss for our overreaction, when in fact, the present situation is just another door for a fly to come in and join the whole swarm of bees that are already nesting inside.

That anxiety attack isn't because you have a big exam next Thursday. It may have its roots in being abandoned by your father. That inability to try new things isn't just you being picky. Its roots are connected to an unexpected move you had to make during college. Certain smells make you nauseous? They may be related to a memory of abuse. It's not that we are seeking out trauma or "digging" for things, but we do want to look at our behaviors, addictions and conflicts and ask, "Is this related to something deeper?"

A good place to start is to keep track of reactions that are seemingly out of balance with a given event. Commit this to memory: **Whenever I respond in a manner which is out of balance to a given situation, there is most likely an area of trauma or sin connected to it.**

For example - Your husband is late getting home from work and forgets to call and let you know. Instead of texting and asking if he's okay, you start down a mental barrage of all the places he could be. Your thoughts veer down the path of, "Is he in a car wreck, is he unfaithful?" or other worried thoughts. By the time he gets home, you have yourself wrapped in an emotional fantasy-land of scenarios which are filled with fear, accusation or even anger. He comes in with an "I'm sorry I ran late" and you go into attack mode with all the different scenarios that have played in your mind for the past hour. He is taken aback by your anger and then quips back with a sarcastic remark and the fight ensues.

Although difficult at times, when you feel yourself overreacting, attempt to ask yourself, "What am I really upset about? What is this connected to?" Stop and ask God to begin to reveal patterns in your life where there may be lies and or trauma which have laid the groundwork for issues such as fear, anxiety, rage and shame to enter in.

When we begin to unravel trauma, it is important to understand where the open doors are. As you progress in your journey you may realize that these woundings or open doors actually have a demonic spirit attached. This is not the focus of this chapter. If you find that after following the steps of the course that you are still plagued with ongoing torment in a particular area, it would be advisable to seek out a prayer team with an understanding of deliverance. We will go into greater detail about this subject in level two of this course.

Recognizing trauma in our lives requires us to look at all aspects of our emotional, physical and spiritual health. This goes beyond our emotional responses. Any area where peace is lacking may be an area that needs to be addressed.

Certainly, no one's life is stress free and always peaceful. However, what you are looking for are patterns of reaction that indicate that something deeper is at work. If we simply view physical issues or diagnosis as isolated components rather than the intricate inner workings of our body, soul and spirit we unwittingly compartmentalize our experiences. Understanding the connections between our spiritual, emotional and physical health is a key component to allowing the Holy Spirit access to heal us on all levels.

So how does trauma affect us? This is by far a non-exhaustive list:

01   Replaying mental images

02   Nightmares

03   Digestive issues

Taking the Thought Captive

This is perhaps one of the most important statements in the entire curriculum. You must learn to take your thoughts captive unto the knowledge of Christ. Memorize II Corinthians 10:5, "We demolish arguments and every pretension that sets itself up against the knowledge of God, and we take captive every thought to make it obedient to Christ."

It is no mistake that this language is somewhat militant. You are in a war, and you must take authority over your mind. This is where the battle begins. What we believe is what we feel and what we feel is what we act upon. If we do not govern our mind by taking authority over it, we will be ruled by it. We all have doubts from time to time, but those pestering thoughts that camp out in our brain that then become tormenting....those are the ones we must wrap up and bring to the knowledge or obedience of Christ.

What does that mean? It means that we speak directly to the lie - we confront it with truth and we command it to leave. When the enemy is no longer able to bombard us in our thought life, he stops. It's not worth it to him. For those of you who are bombarded daily with thoughts of suicide, depression, anxiety or self-loathing as examples, the battle can be exhausting at first. You will need to build up your muscles to fight this battle, but you can do it.

We need to grab hold of and take captive thoughts that don't line up with the Word

An example of taking a thought captive:

Scenario 1: Every time you walk into a new environment you immediately think people are talking about you or rejecting you. You don't fit in, you're too.....old, young, poor, fat or whatever the lie is. You miss the main activity because you are fixated on how anxious you feel about being rejected or judged.

Scenario 2: You get a call telling you that your high school son was picked up for drug use at school. You spend the phone call beating yourself up for being a bad parent. You can't hear anything the principal is saying because this all reflects on you. You're divorced, you work long hours and this is all your fault.

In either situation perhaps there is some level of truth. Maybe you are being judged or rejected, or maybe you haven't been a great parent, but being caught up in the accusation of the enemy is paralyzing. Dwelling there will never lead to freedom. If there is sin - forgive it. Forgive God, yourself and others, but then address the LIE.

Scenario #1 *Father, I bring You the lie that I am always rejected. I know that You accept me. I ask that You would cover me in Your presence and help me to find my identity in You and You alone. Jesus, fill those places that long for the approval of others. God, you said that I am fearfully and wonderfully made. I choose to walk in Your identity. I reject a spirit of rejection and come out of agreement with the enemy.*

Scenario #2 *Jesus, I ask that You help me to see how to best help my son in this situation. Father, I acknowledge that I feel shame in this situation, but that is not Your heart towards me or my son. I bring shame and accusation to the feet of Jesus, and I choose to walk in the truth that He is for me and not against me.*

Your sleyhook is ready for you to begin wielding it, to pull in wayward threads. Identifying that the voice or thought you are dwelling on is actually often the voice of the enemy can be a process in and of itself. Of course, we too can speak lies over ourselves, but most often, just like with Eve, the lie is planted by the enemy. It could be the words, "Curse God," "Be like God," or the myriad of other lies that he throws our way. Once you become adept at identifying the voice of the enemy you will be surprised at how predictable he is. You see, Satan is not a creator, he is an imitator. He does not give identity, he attempts to steal it.

So, pull out that sleyhook— and capture some lies.

For those who walk in the flesh, we do not war according to the flesh. For the weapons of our warfare are not carnal but mighty in God for pulling down strongholds, casting down arguments and vain imaginations and everything that exalts itself against the knowledge of God, bringing every thought into captivity to the obedience of Christ. 2 Corinthians 10:3-5 (NKJ)

Perch and Scour

Jesus - I desire to live in truth. I know I can bring the tormenting accusations and lies to You. I need Your help to show me the lies I do not easily recognize. Please show me areas where Your truth does not permeate my thoughts and emotions. I ask that You would convict me of reactions that lack self-control or where I pick up offense.

I confess that sometimes my mind runs away with thoughts and lies that take me away from Your peace. Help me to receive Your healing instead of staying isolated with tormenting images and memories. I bring each of those to You and ask that You would reveal the truth behind each lie.

Where I do not know the truth, I give You permission to teach. I submit my mind, will and emotions to the process of sanctification.

06

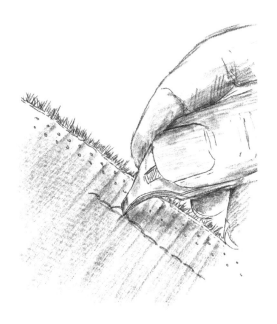

Chapter 06

Untangling the Knots: Guilt, Shame, Regret and Grief

> *The burls can be removed from your life by His Hand applying His burling tool*

The knots of guilt, shame, regret and grief typically hang out together, often binding together and strengthening one another over time. We metaphorically refer to these troublesome burls as the "Knot Brothers". These four partner with nearly every traumatic event that we experience. The strength of their lies and accusations can be some of the most difficult to untangle. While not always the case, there can be an element of truth which allows the knots to intermingle, intensifying the confusion and torment.

The Knot Brothers are most often the voices lurking in the closet behind our most tormenting thoughts. They know us well, and as such, are able to attach themselves to strands of our identity and purpose. They are those little comments as you enter a room or conversation, or the overwhelming persistent ones that keep us from running to Jesus. They often are such a constant companion that we often think they are actually part of our authentic self.

> *Shame, regret, grief and guilt are emotions that can push themselves into our lives when we have experienced trauma*

Their self-dialogue can be subtle or tormenting and because they are so familiar, we allow them to just hang out with us. Until we recognize these knots as distractions and hindrances to the beauty of the tapestry that is being woven, they hinder our relationships, our calling and our ability to be at peace with what God is weaving. Understanding the role of these nasty accusers can help you to eliminate a common open door of the enemy. The quicker we recognize these knots, the sooner we are able to cut them off and keep them from distorting the threads of our true identity. The ability to recognize these voices as foreign to our own voice, is essential in addressing the lies that the enemy attempts to weave in. Time for some 'burling" to happen.

Guilt is often a very misunderstood emotion. As one that is God-given, its purpose is to lead us to conviction by the Holy Spirit and then to repentance and finally to receive forgiveness. Unfortunately, if we have not been discipled correctly or we have a cycle of shame and guilt in our childhood, we often get stuck in the process, never arriving at the destination of repentance and forgiveness. Our response to guilt is crucial to which pathway we choose to walk. One path ends in freedom and the other leads to torment and shame that can leave us looking backward with regret for large portions of our lives.

Guilt occurs when we have knowingly done something wrong, and we take responsibility for it. An example would be taking money off the table at a restaurant left behind for the waitress or telling our boss that we were sick yesterday, when actually we were playing golf with some buddies. Both of these actions break basic commandments and the impetus behind each was a deliberate choice. The corresponding feeling that should accompany such behaviors for a believer should be conviction. This gift of conviction, given by the Holy Spirit, allows us to know when we have grieved the heart of the Father and broken/ damaged relationship with Him. When we continually sin, we can "harden our hearts" to the voice of the Holy Spirit and thus not feel "conviction." 2 Corinthians 7:10 says that, "Godly sorrow brings repentance that leads to salvation and leaves no regret, but worldly sorrow brings death."

Unfortunately, feeling guilt and being guilty are not always the same thing. We can and often do feel guilty for things we did NOT do or did not do purposely. Depending on our personalities, upbringing and how this emotion was levied in our family of origin, some of us can FEEL guilty for just about ANYTHING. Take a moment and list 3 things you feel guilty about that WERE your responsibility. Be honest...own them. They can be small, seemingly insignificant things.

01

....
....
....
....
....
....

02

....
....
....
....
....
....

03

....
....
....
....
....

Now list 3 things that you feel guilty about that were out of your control or were not your fault at all.

01

....
....
....
....
....

02

....
....
....
....
....

03

....
....
....
....
....

When guilt is used as a weapon by our family of origin, relationally or by the enemy it can quickly spiral into shame, the second voice. He is like the silent twin that follows guilt around, waiting for the right time to step in and introduce himself. For shame is the ugliest of the 4 voices because he points not at WHAT we did but WHO we are. Guilt says *"I did this.....it was bad."* Shame says, *"I did this....I am bad."* This subtle difference can wreak havoc on the way we mature and self-identify. Entire family structures can be built on lies of shame. We will deal with this later in the chapter, but for now know that shame doesn't just accuse, it blames. This nasty emotion is often used by abusers to weaponize their attacks on their victims. It is used as conditioning to control for it is powerful.

When shame is used as a weapon, its victim will dance to the yielding of its blade. Ever been in a relationship where everything is "your fault?" After time, this lie has you believing that you can do nothing correctly, indicating that you have taken on shame as an identity. An abusive partner hits you and says he only did it because "you make him angry." Over time, the victim begins to believe this nonsense and identifies so strongly with shame that she loses her ability to self-advocate and remove herself from an obviously damaging relationship. Shame can make us feel depressed, passive and constantly in the shadows.

How do you recognize this vile, passive voice? Do you often respond to situations with, "It's probably my fault?" Do you make excuses for spouses, bosses or children who treat you poorly? Do you often find yourself thinking "I deserve this or that because of what I did?" Those are all the voices of shame.

Shame is often a difficult web to unravel when it is a thematic presence in our lives. Recognizing its voice and pattern is the first step to applying the burling iron, pulling out the threads, piece by piece.

Often interwoven amidst shame and guilt is our other "knot" .....regret. Regret can hit us, making us feel powerless, for it is always something that seems

01   Are you able to distinguish between mistakes you've made and WHO you are?

02   Have you taken on shame about being abused or mistreated?

03   Does your family of origin carry shame about any particular issue?

"unchangeable." It is passed and done. Regret can open the door to both guilt or shame, but often works alone as well. Regret can be based on actions that we did commit or on actions that we failed to commit, or omission. I can feel regret because I forgot someone's birthday or regret that I said hasty words to my father before he passed away.

Regrets come in two categories. Regrets of **omission** - something I didn't do and should have done or **commission,** things we have done. Regret does not necessarily attach itself to an act of sin. It can be attached to decisions, relationships, words spoken and on and on. Often these are things we cannot change. The enemy knows this and attaches regret to the event or decision. Regret often walks in just in front of guilt and shame for he is a door keeper. For example:

A   I regret that I was working so much when my children were younger.

B   I feel guilty because my son struggles in school so much, because I was not around to support him

C   I feel shame that I am a bad parent for not being the parent that he needed.

List 3 regrets of omission: Try to make these different from your answers about guilt.

01

02

03

List 3 regrets of commission:

01

02

03

Have you walked through self-forgiveness with each of these regrets?

Why or why not?

Guilt, shame and regret often hang out together like 3 masked amigos. They can look a lot alike until we unmask and understand what is at work. Because the 3 amigos are so cunning at how they team up and bully the believer, we want to take some time to unmask the most common tactics they use. Here are some of the most common lies. See if you can readily relate to these common accusations:

01   It was my responsibility. I should have,
      I could have.....

02   I didn't try hard enough, stay long enough,
      communicate well enough.....

03   If I had fought back.

04   If I had told someone sooner.

05   I deserve to be treated this way because......

Applying biblical principles to the areas of guilt, shame and regret are essential to the healing journey of trauma recovery.

01   You are only responsible for actions that you
      knowingly committed. You cannot repent for a
      sin you didn't commit.

02   You are not responsible for someone else's
      response, if you did not sin. This will often
      happen when we begin to set personal
      boundaries.

03   When I repent and ask forgiveness, I am truly
      forgiven. When the enemy brings it up again -
      that is his accusation, not my truth.

04   I may have done something bad, but I am NOT
      bad. I am fearfully and wonderfully made by
      God who loves me dearly.

05   Is the emotion I am experiencing driving me to
      God or away from him?

06   Guilt, shame and regret all lead to nowhere,
      they are stagnant emotions.

We quoted earlier 2 Corinthians 7:10 but let's look at it this time in the Message translation. *"Distress that drives us to God does that. It turns us around. It gets us back in the way of salvation. We never regret that kind of pain. But those who let distress drive them away from God are full of regrets and end up on a deathbed of regrets."*

If we are unfamiliar with the true nature and character of God, either from a lack of discipleship or a lifetime of poor examples by our fathers, often we are not aware of the kindness and goodness of God. Romans 2:4 explains that it is the kindness of God that LEADS us to repentance. It is not His hand of judgment or punishment, but the open arms of a Father.

If we have never experienced that type of embrace from a father when we've done something wrong, we've repented and been forgiven, the process can become clogged with hurdles, because we don't understand the nature and character of God. It is important as you heal to not put the limitations of your own experiences on God. Our experiences with people do not define or limit who God is, but they can certainly hinder OUR ability to receive and connect.

God's purpose is NEVER condemnation - that is the voice of the accuser or our own voice or the voice of others. Feeling guilt or shame is NOT the same as repenting and the enemy knows that. If he can keep us in the cycle of simply "feeling bad", we will never move toward repentance and freedom.

01   Repent if needed or speak truth to the accusation

02   Forgive God, yourself and others

03   Ask for healing in your mind, body and spirit

It is the accuser's job to bring accusations against you, both the true and the false, but it is God's job to defend you. He is the witness in your trial and he is also the judge, a righteous judge. *"Yet the Lord longs to be gracious to you; therefore He will rise up to show you compassion. For the Lord is a God of justice. Blessed are all who wait for him,"* Isaiah 30:18. Romans 8 tells us that there is no condemnation in Christ Jesus and finally in Psalm 103:8 God tells us that He is slow to anger, abounding in love and grace toward us. If these statements meet resistance in your spirit, spend some time meditating on their truths. Ask the Lord to show you why you have a hard time believing this to be true about Him.

Where and when did you start believing a lie about the goodness of God? Has it always been there? Did it happen after a particular event? Were you taught this?

Weeping May Endure For a Night

Grief - Because grief is shared universally, particularly around the subject of death, there are great resources which have been written on this topic. For our purposes we will focus primarily on the stages of grief that if we don't move past them, can cause us to end up in a state of bondage. Let us preface that there is a **holy grief.** This progression helps us heal after the death of a loved one, the loss of a relationship or grieving another significant loss. Remember, weeping may endure for a night, but joy comes in the morning. Grief can take time, but during this time, we need to keep a close watch over our soul so that we do not open the door for things to attach to us, which can greatly prolong the cycle of grief and at its worst, derail us spiritually.

Let's face it, dealing with loss is not easy. Whether it is an unfulfilled expectation or the loss of a loved one, grief can pack a powerful punch. It is often unpredictable, making us feel completely out of control of our emotions and sense of normalcy. There is an injustice to loss that is extremely hard to navigate on our own without the help of the Holy Spirit. When we do not allow the Lord to navigate this path for us, we end up with unresolved grief which is often the source of depression, anxiety and misplaced anger. Grief is a response to our anticipated outcome not developing as we planned. It can come swiftly, with no regard for our feelings. We can't bargain it away. Grief is a journey that must be walked through.

Grief is marked by loss. It may be the loss of innocence, security, a loved one or physical security like a job or home. Due to the injustice of grief, we can experience a firestorm of emotions raging from anger, fear, sadness, and loneliness just to name a few. Grief is not tidy. There are not 1, 2, 3 microwave steps. In your workbook you will see the grief journey mapped out. Unlike the popular self-help books that model the stages of grief, in reality, the path looks much more akin to the scribbling of a two-year-old.

Because the emotions associated with grief are so intense, many of us will avoid grief altogether. Understandably, the road is not an easy one. However, if we do not stay on the path and instead choose to take a detour, we will find ourselves in the middle of the desert, wishing we hadn't gone "offroading." If you stay on the path, you may encounter roadblocks, construction and delays, but this is a road that you want to stay on and arrive at the destination, healed and finding the goodness of God that does manifest on the other side of grief.

The stages of grief have been written about in multiple formats. If you are unfamiliar with these steps, take time to familiarize yourself.

1. Denial - This is the most common response to loss. It acts as a defense mechanism and helps to buffer shock at the traumatic experience.

2. Anger - The result of extreme pain or discomfort, this manifestation occurs because it is typically more socially acceptable than expressing fear.

3. Bargaining - This is the stage where one begins to barter the pain away through negotiation.

4. Depression - This is the place of reality, where the depth of the loss is felt.

5. Acceptance - At this stage, the individual resists the urge to deny or change their situation. There is an understanding of the gravity of loss.

These stages are not sequential and can twist and repeat throughout the journey, as referenced in the chart here and in the workbook. But what about other blocks to navigating grief? There are significant reactions or behaviors that can cause us to get stuck in the grief cycle. Grief, when navigated by the Holy Spirit leads us to Jesus, to His comfort and His direction. When we allow ourselves to divert the holy process of grief we can inadvertently lengthen or halt the process altogether. As you attempt to forge your journey with grief, keep these following challenges in front of you to check in periodically to make sure you are not being derailed.

Isolation

Isolation can be tricky. Grief can be awkward. We've all been there. What do we say? What do we not say? Do we talk about the issue at hand or do we try to navigate around it? These relational hurdles can cause the person who is in the walk of grief to pull back and isolate. You don't want to be a burden and everyone else has seemingly moved on. Everyone is ready for you to be "done" and well quite honestly, you are not, so rather than play the emotional tug of war, you remove yourself. This unhealthy reaction at a time when you need community can be avoided by seeking counseling and surrounding yourself with people who will allow you to acknowledge your pain and move through it in any given situation.

Enshrinement

This occurs when we process our grief by making the person or situation that we've lost into the symbol of perfection, without the balance of reality. We begin to create multiple anniversary celebrations and rituals around their lives. Everything is about honoring them, with little to no account for their human frailties and dispositions. This can be caused by guilt, over not resolving relational conflict before the death or it can be a purposeful act to brush up what we know could be a tarnished story. If we create the expectation on ourselves or others that everything we now do must somehow "honor the legacy" of the one who died, then we are placing undue stress and expectation on ourselves and others.

Certainly, we do not want to use one's death as a time to point out someone's imperfections as that would be cruel. However, if there were unfinished conversations or relational strains, we cannot adequately work through the grief process if we are not dealing with real emotions. At best, we will move through the process superficially, leaving gaping holes in the healing because it is clouded in deception.

Creating a Monster

In stark opposition to enshrinement, we can also create a scenario in which the deceased is characterized as a heinous monster with little to no redemptive qualities. This is more common in scenarios involving trauma victims, ex-spouses or broken relationships for example. We characterize the person solely by their actions toward us and we take away their humanity. This creates distance between us and the deceased. This is an avoidant tactic. Again, honestly looking at the humanity of the person with their faults, will help us to honestly grieve any level of relationship loss that was present.

Replacement

This blockage is often a learned behavior. It is a coping mechanism that is touted in many families. Imagine the scenario where a kitten dies unexpectedly. The child is of course distraught. In an effort to cope with the loss, the family rushes out to purchase another kitten. Such replacement teaches us...don't grieve, don't feel the sadness, just move on with a new pet. We can utilize this faulty mechanism with sports teams, unfulfilled goals, church relationships and the like. Don't stop to grieve it, just replace it. The problem is we cannot grieve what we do not acknowledge as loss.

The timeline of grief is different for everyone. As we work through our grief timeline, be honest with the feelings you may have suppressed and give yourself permission to grieve even the smallest of things. So how do you know when you have grieved well? If you are able to think of the person with happy past memories rather than overwhelming present emotion, that is a good sign. If what you are grieving is not a person, but something less tangible such as innocence or security you can ask yourself, "Am I able to look at what was lost and say that despite this, I have adapted and am now flourishing?"

The knots of shame, guilt, regret and grief often weave together, creating strongholds which warp our identity. Most importantly they stand as an interference to receiving the Father's love and are some of the most common lies the enemy uses to torment. Recognizing these false friends can speed up our healing process. It is important to realize that due to the strength of these particular lies we cannot simply acknowledge that we see them at work but must literally pull them out of our tapestry for they need to be replaced with new threads of truth.

Perch and Scour

Father, I bring to You my shame. I acknowledge that it is the part of me that is most hidden. I give You permission to shine your light on my hiddenness. Where there are areas of regret, I bring those events to You and lay them at Your feet, to never again pick them up. I know that the guilt that I feel must be released.

Help me to completely receive the fullness of Your forgiveness and help me to forgive myself. I know that Your forgiveness is not earned, it is a free gift. Jesus, I embrace the process of letting shame, regret and grief go. I commit to the journey of healing and removing each of these knots, one at a time.

Jesus, please help me to rightly discern between guilt and conviction. I welcome the conviction of the Holy Spirit in my life, but I reject the accusations of guilt and shame. Please quicken my spirit to quickly see the difference.

Father, I bring You any remaining grief I may be stuck in. Help me to be honest about any unholy grief. If there is grief in my past regarding an event or personal loss that I have not yet processed, please bring that and the depth of the accompanying pain to my memory so that I may release that to You properly and fully.

Jesus, I thank You that You alone are my Comforter. Show me the depths of Your love and care for my heart and the areas that are raw and open. Help me to take the time to allow You to love me and establish Your truth in my inmost parts.

07

Chapter 07

The Ties That Bind

For those raised in the church, the familiar hymn, Blessed Be The Tie That Binds is all too fitting for this chapter. Look at a few of the most memorable verses penned by John Fawcett in 1782.

Blest Be the Tie that binds

Our hearts in Christian love

The fellowship of kindred minds

Is like to that above

Before Our Father's throne

We pour our ardent prayers

Our fears, our hopes, our aims are one

Our comforts and our cares

We share our mutual woes

Our mutual burdens bear

And often for each other flows

The sympathizing tear

The Bible refers to bonds throughout scripture. Interestingly enough, in Hebrew, the same word used for *bond* is the same word as *ligament*. It is literally that which holds the bones together. God is a relational God. Connection is important to Him. He created us for relationship with Himself and with others. The enemy knows this and does everything He can to thwart and taint our relationships. This destruction then further supports lies that we believe about our self-worth, about abandonment and hope for our future.

There has been much recent research on the topic of community as a necessary component of addiction recovery. Many call addiction the disease of **loneliness**. This research was supported by the astronomical 30% increase in drug overdoses as well as suicide attempts during the Covid Pandemic quarantines. In some states the rates increased by 40%. *We were created for* **RELATIONSHIP**. When we have secure attachment to God, ourselves and others, we are attached to the loom. The weaving process can stretch us, but we stay connected. What do your primary relationships look like? Are they fraught with codependency, enmeshment and conflict?

Imagine a loom where the tapestry is haphazardly attached to the ties. Occasional pins are missed completely, or the tie-offs are so loose that even with the slightest pressure the warp disconnects and the tapestry falls to the ground.

This is much the same with our attachment style. If we do not experience secure attachment as a child, we will develop faulty attachment styles that follow us well into adulthood. Attachment and security are essential elements for healing.

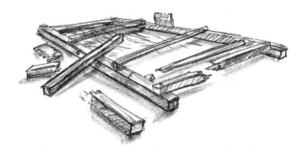

We (our 'loom') can become 'broken' if we did not experience good attachment as a child

We have spent the bulk of this journey discussing our relationship with God and the lies we believe. We now turn to addressing how our wounds affect our relationships with others. For some, wounding has caused us to isolate and become overly self-dependent, refusing to embrace our need for others and for community, while for others unhealthy attachments and patterns plague nearly every relationship we have, keeping us in a constant state of reactivity. Neither extreme is healthy. Our attachments are most secure when we are anchored in Christ. Our stability in connection with the Father allows us to love without unhealthy expectation. Devoid from our identity being rooted in Him, we seek to be validated or rescued by our relationships instead of enjoying the beautiful freedom that Christ intended for us.

Before we launch into defining many different aspects of unhealthy bonds and attachments, it is necessary to define what healthy relationships look like. Often with histories of abuse and lack of attachment, it is possible that a person has never experienced a healthy attachment which further keeps them in the cycle of unhealthy bondage. Loving relationships are marked by safety, honesty, mutual respect, trust, and accountability.

A traumatic bonding can occur between a victim and a perpetrator. This may be as simple as a relationship where one person carries significantly more power. Often periods of reward or positive reinforcements follow cycles of mental or physical abuse. The perpetrator then apologizes or shows remorse and attempts to repair the relationship.

Signs of trauma bonding

:: The person becomes extremely affectionate, very quickly

:: Exaggerated gestures such as proposing, declarations of intimacy in a very short time frame

:: Jealousy and suspicion veiled as "caring"

:: Lack of boundaries

:: Extreme highs and lows

:: A loss of self in the relationship

:: Gaslighting

:: Making excuses for the abuser

Soul Ties - Knitted Together

A soul tie refers to an intense emotional or physical connection. This depth of connection can keep one feeling in bondage to a person. Often unholy soul ties are addressed when sexual intimacy is involved. This is one reason sexual sin has such a profound effect on someone. When sex outside of marriage occurs, it breaks the holy biblical principle of two becoming one flesh.

There is a union which takes places that affects the person's mind, soul and body. In weaving we call this 'blending'. Two different fibres are blended together in one yarn which results in a mixture and blending of the two and a combined color mixture. You are doing this when you become emotionally or physically tied to someone else – a part of their nature becomes a part of yours and vice versa.

Parts of us can become 'tied' in a soul tie to someone else - in an unhealthy way

It is always wise to pray for soul ties to be broken between sexual partners, even if this includes casual sex or forced sexual encounters. Because of the intimate nature of the violation, a soul tie can occur, even when one person is not engaged emotionally. Much like the scripture which states that the two shall become one flesh, blending takes two or more fibers and weaves them together in a new homogenous fiber. This is done to create certain fiber characteristics which are unobtainable from a single fiber, such as strength, elasticity or sheen.

This can be a beautiful process resulting in a stronger, more desired fiber when the blended yarns are pure and have desirable characteristics. One would never purposely blend a yarn which was stained, impure or defective. While people are never perfect, the understanding of "blending" that occurs spiritually when a sexual tie or union is created should cause one to be extremely cautious about sexual ties and encounters.

Soul ties can also occur in intimate friendships as well as to places and things. Not all soul ties are ungodly. As the body of Christ, we are to be 'bonded and rooted' in love. As in the relationship of Jonathan and David in 1 Samuel 18 it reads: "After David had finished talking with Saul, Jonathan became one in spirit with David, and he loved him as himself." However, if the relationship is marked with codependency or manipulation and bondage, it is no longer a holy tie.

How do you determine if your friendship or relationship has an unholy soul tie?

01   Preoccupation with the person or believing there is a "special connection." Any type of obsession with the relationship.

02   Feeling the person's presence with you, when they are not present.

03   Vows and covenants that were not directed by God.

04   You excuse manipulation, bullying or mistreatment from this person.

To Break a Soul Tie

01 Repent

02 Renounce

03 Forgive

04 Be aware of items, trinkets and things
    connected to the person or place that the Lord
    may ask you to get rid of

Enmeshment - A strand of two is easily broken

Enmeshment is defined loosely as an extreme form of closeness between individuals. The term most often occurs in family units. However it can take place in social and romantic relationships as well. Enmeshment is established when there are very low levels of autonomy coupled with low boundaries which results in inappropriate levels of intimacy.

In the family unit this occurs when intergenerational bonding is skewed because the child becomes a surrogate spouse for the mother/father. The child becomes the fixer and often responsible for the emotional stability of the parent. Other situations involve family norms where personal boundaries are not respected or are non-existent. The family unit takes on the emotional angst of any individual family member or the parents live their lives vicariously through the activities and relationships of the child.

Codependency

Relationships are meant to be mutually satisfying. Typically, in the codependent situation one person manifests low self-esteem and a strong desire for approval coupled with another, more dominant personality, which exhibits manipulation and control. This results in one becoming dependent on the needs or the control of another.

Summed up, it is a relationship where one person is the "caretaker" and the other person takes advantage. This severe imbalance of power can seem appropriate in the beginning and often goes unchecked until the woven threads of manipulation and strangulation are the hallmarks of the relationship.

It is easy to point the finger at the person in the more dominant and manipulative role, but the truth is both are wounded. The loss of self and attempting to find identity by fixing others is not noble. This relational weaving most often occurs in families that have experienced addiction. However it can occur in any relationship dynamic where one person lays down personal boundaries in an attempt to save the other. There are multiple counseling resources available for those struggling with codependency, but for this study, addressing the roots of control, idolatry and low self-worth are the foundational lies that need to be addressed.

Bitter Root Judgments

There are two Greek words for judgment in the Bible, and both are translated with the same English word.

> 1. "But he who is spiritual judges all things . . ." I Cor. 2:5. The word translated "judges" in this verse is anakrino in Greek which means to investigate.
>
> 2. Mat. 7:1-2 "Do not judge, or you too will be judged. For in the same way you judge others, you will be judged, and with the measure you use, it will be measured to you." The word "judge" here is the Greek word krino which means to put on trial or to condemn.

Wounding, particularly the wounds of childhood, often result in judgments which are made by an immature agreement for control or protection. Left alone, these judgments grow beneath the surface, often undetected until the fruit is abundant because bitter root judgments are often made from a place of helplessness and victimization. Feeling unprotected, unloved or objectified, the child garners their inner strength to create invisible walls of self-protection.

Here are verses addressing bitter root judgments, to shed more light on them:

Heb. 12:15 *"See to it that no one falls short of the grace of God and that no bitter root grows up to cause trouble and defile many."*

Jas. 2:12-13 *"... judgment without mercy will be shown to anyone who has not been merciful. Mercy triumphs over judgment!"*

Deut 5:16 *"Honor your father and your mother, as the Lord your God has commanded you, so that you may live long and that it may go well with you in the land the Lord your God is giving you."*

How do these judgments manifest subconsciously or consciously?

:: Judgment against those who should have protected us, resulting in viewing them as stupid, uncaring, unloving, weak or worthy of punishment.

:: Self judgment of being ugly, bad, unlovable or stupid. We may make an agreement with death.

:: Judgment of God as being cruel, absent or punitive.

It seems unjust or unfair that a child would be held accountable for decisions made out of self-preservation. The problem is these initial thoughts become beliefs, then actions and eventually sin. **We are always responsible for our reaction to sin, even when we are the victim.**

The Problem with Judging

:: Biblical Principle: *"Do not judge, and you will not be judged. Do not condemn, and you will not be condemned. Forgive, and you will be forgiven. ... For with the measure you use, it will be measured to you."* Luke 6:37-38

:: Biblical Principle: *"Do not be deceived: God cannot be mocked. A man reaps what he sows. Whoever sows to please their flesh, from the flesh will reap destruction; whoever sows to please the Spirit, from the Spirit will reap eternal life.""* Gal. 6:7-8

If we sow judgment, we will reap judgment. When we judge others, we are dooming ourselves, because we WILL do the things for which we have condemned others.

:: Biblical Principle: *"There is only one Lawgiver and Judge."* Jas. 4:12

We are not God, and He does not look kindly on it, when we position ourselves in His seat.

Application

Is it the heart of the Father for us to be wounded and harmed and simply take it, without response? Do we always just turn the other cheek? Do we just accept sin done against us? No, we are free to judge the behavior, but we are not to judge the person or God.

"A person's own folly leads to their ruin, yet their heart rages against the Lord."
Prov. 19:3

Bitter Root Expectations

Often when negative things happen repeatedly, we begin to expect the worst. This bitter root can affect us and those around us. This expectation actually has soul power which can elicit behaviors from people contrary to how they would normally behave.

We project our expectation upon them, thereby defiling them as referenced in Hebrews 12:15, "See to it that no one falls short of the grace of God and that no bitter root grows up to cause trouble and defile many." This pattern is often seen in the lives of persons who are repeatedly abused physically and or sexually. There can be other components such as demonic spirit attachment, but it is good to start with our own expectations to lessen the opportunity for these open doors.

If you find yourself seeing repeated relationship patterns of abuse, betrayal, infidelity or other negative patterns, be mindful to chart these in your trauma timeline as areas to address.

Inner Vows

Inner Vows are typically motivated by bitter root judgments or a desire to self-protect. An inner vow is powered by the soul or even self-righteous determination. These inner vows can isolate us with walls we don't even want to be there, but the agreement was made so long ago, we don't even see its beginning.

Inner vows imprison us to think and act based on the vow's intent

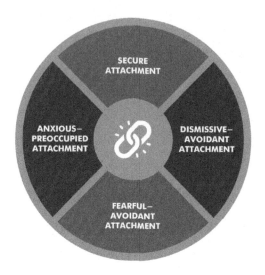

Attachment Styles

There are four major types of attachment styles. These can be difficult to self-analyze, because we often do not see our own areas of weakness. Attachment is so intrinsically woven into our very being that often we just see these relational styles as "just who I am." If we are to securely attach to God, ourselves and others, we must honestly access our ability to create healthy bonds of attachment.

This is not an attempt to assume that everyone has the same level of need for attachment. However, if feelings of isolation, self-worth and self -defense are the motivators for your current relationships, a further look into the episodic and thematic wounds affecting your ability to securely bond are worthy of your consideration.

Secure Attachment

The healthiest of styles is the secure attachment. These people are comfortable connecting with others as well as asking for help or support when they need it.

They are able to share emotions in a healthy way. They do not default to rejection or fear of abandonment when there is conflict. Personal worth is acknowledged.

Dismissive-Avoidant Attachment

People with this type of attachment style (also known as insecure - avoidant) are often those who have experienced neglect or consistent rejection from caregivers. These people are typically extremely independent. They avoid close connections with others. They are often secret keepers in an effort to maintain their independence.

Fearful-Avoidant Attachment

Abuse, chaos and neglect may lead to this type of attachment style. This is most typical when the primary caregivers were the ones who inflicted the pain. As adults, these persons are often afraid to be alone, but also exhibit fear with regard to closeness and intimacy. The inability to trust is pivotal in that they will often alternate between a "clingy" connection or complete avoidance.

Anxious-Preoccupied Attachment

These persons respond to the inconsistencies between attention and coldness in their childhood experience by developing a preoccupation or hypersensitivity to any changes in their current relationship. They may present as very needy, clingy or obsessive about their partners. This intensity level can often be too much for people and the person ends up with a self-fulfilling prophecy of abandonment.

There is a lot of information to process in this chapter. You may find that all or little of it applies to your personal situation. Adjusting these ties to our framework is an essential step to finding freedom with others. Take as much time as you need to process through this information and refer to it often throughout your healing journey.

Perch and Scour

Jesus, I bring to You any persons that I have had sexual intimacy with. It is my desire to cut all soul ties with anyone other than my spouse. I ask that You sever all sexual ties and any emotional soul ties that occurred as a result of these unions. Father, I ask that You cleanse my mind, body and emotions from all unholy connections with this person. Father, I forgive this person for any violation that may have occurred or that was against my will.

Please remove memories, flashbacks and emotional connections to these times of sexual union, desired or not. Father, I release all of my former sexual partners to You. I release control, vengeance, memories and desire.

Father, I bring to You any relationships that have created unholy soul ties through intimate conversation and sharing or bonds created through trauma. I ask that the bonds that we share would only be holy and pure. If I have engaged in manipulation or control in a relationship, please forgive me and I release this person to you. I release memories and soulish attachments that would draw us together in an unholy way.

Father, I acknowledge that the words of my heart and the meditations of my heart are powerful. I bring to You the following inner vows that I have made about myself, God and others. I repent of self-protection and using my soul power to control my surroundings and relationships. Jesus, help me to begin to trust You as my protector.

I repent for inner judgments that I have made that ultimately hurt me. Please show me areas of hidden agreements that I may have even made in my childhood that have affected the path and experiences of my life. Jesus, I repent of judging my parents or others in authority over me, even if their actions were not always appropriate. I choose to honor the position they hold in my life as parents. Show me how to truly forgive and honor, even if a mutual relationship is not possible at this time. I choose, as an act of my will, to walk in forgiveness and freedom with regard to all relationships, knowing that You Jesus are the only judge.

08

Chapter 08

Cut from a
Different Cloth

The idiom "cut from a different cloth," refers to one who is different from the rest. As believers seeking healing, we are called to be different. We cannot take the measures and expectations of the world and expect them to line up with the principles and truths of a living God. His ways are higher; His healing greater than any therapy or method on earth.

The wisdom of God can at times be foolish to men. No greater demonstration of that tension is seen than when we look at the threads of forgiveness and repentance. Because the world has not experienced the forgiveness of God, they do not understand the power of forgiveness in our relationships, and because the world does not know or accept absolute truth, they are reluctant to call us to repent.

As we have addressed in several chapters before, unforgiveness of God, self and others can be a legal right for the enemy to attack and torment. It breaks the very principle upon which God sacrificed His Son, Jesus. It is that important. His death is in vain if we do not repent. It is a gift that goes unused. As believers we know that our repentance and God's forgiveness of our sins is the foundation upon which all other Biblical truth is bound. We are not in and of ourselves able to save ourselves. However, if we are not careful, we can build a sin-based theology. What do I mean by that?

First of all, let's clarify that we are not adding or taking away from scripture here. You MUST repent to be saved and forgiven. However, if our theology stops at the aspect of repentance versus repentance that culminates in fulfilled healing, we can fall short of all God has intended for us. Repentance can become a ritual, an expected deed when we've done wrong. We never want to become hardened to the voice of the Holy Spirit or conviction, but what happens when we continually repent and there is no change? This is often what happens in the cycle of addiction.

Even if one is able to escape the endless cycle of shame that can accompany addiction or other sin, the emphasis is often placed upon self- motivation, self-control, and behavior modification. None of these are what elicit true healing. Repentance without the spirit of God can lead us into legalism or void religion. Remember, it always takes SPIRIT and TRUTH. Yes, we must repent, but if we are not met with the touch from the Father, often true healing ie fruit, is not seen. This endless cycle of TRY HARDER is exhausting. But how do we engage our spirit with our heavenly Father?

| ***We need to balance the spirit with truth***

> If we apply the logic of man, we are justified in our unforgiveness. Who would expect someone to actually forgive an abusive father, a murderer, a thief?
>
> God does.

It fights against our rational minds, but that is exactly the summation of this curriculum, that our minds and emotions are secondary to the authority and work of our spirit.

Our will is the place of our inner strength. It must be engaged and aligned with the purposes and plan of Christ. We can and we do things in our own strength, but that power is magnified when we submit our will to the strength of the Father. Many times, we will begin prayers with, "As an act of my will..." Sometimes emotionally or with our intellect we are not ready to engage the promises or the actions of obedience, such as forgiveness. Engaging the will so that it comes into agreement with what our spirit wants is part of bringing the body, soul (the mind, will, and emotions) UNDER the authority of our spirit.

The most prevalent word for "forgive" in the New Testament is aphiemi. It means to let go, set free or release. Certainly, letting go of the effects of unforgiveness are appealing. Multiple scientific studies point out that the ability to forgive has dramatic effects on blood pressure, the immune system, anxiety and depression and a reduction of chronic pain.

Forgiveness is a process and can at times need to unravel one thread at a time. Start with your will. Make the choice to forgive, even when emotion or release doesn't follow. Unwrap any lies connected to the person or event. Always start with God, then self, then others. Below are some common areas that we get tripped up in when trying to process forgiveness.

Forgiveness is a foundational requirement for healing

"Bear with each other and forgive one another. If any of you has a grievance against someone forgive as the Lord forgave you." Col 3:13

:: *Biblical forgiveness is not absolving the wrongdoer....that is God's job.*

:: *Biblical forgiveness is not forgetting.*

:: *Biblical forgiveness does not equate with restoration, although that may come.*

:: *Choosing forgiveness is a step of obedience between you and the Father.*

:: *Choosing to forgive releases: resentment, anger and bitterness.*

:: *Choosing to forgive means you stop rehearsing the offense.*

Hindrances to Forgiveness

If God commanded us to forgive, why is it so hard?

:: We want JUSTICE - our flesh response is that we want punishment or at a minimum, acknowledgement of the pain we have suffered. We want our freedom, but we seek retribution for the offender. Forgiveness sacrifices the need to see justice. This too is in God's hands.

:: Self-Righteous - we often view the sins of others more harshly than we view our own sin.

As Paul taught in Ephesians 4:32, we are to learn to forgive as Christ forgives us. If you struggle with forgiveness, look at the lie likely tied around your ability to fully accept God's forgiveness in your own life.

Let's look at God's Forgiveness:

> :: If we confess our sins, He is faithful and just and will forgive us our sins and purify us from all unrighteousness. 1 John 1:9

> :: For I willl forgive their wickedness and will remember their sins no more. Hebrews 8:12

> :: Repent, then, and turn to God, so that your sins may be wiped out, that times of refreshing may come from the Lord. Acts 3:19-20

If you continue to struggle with accepting God's complete and full forgiveness, return to the section on shame and regret. The ability to release all the pain and effects of sin rests on our ability to allow God to carry it for us. Anything less is only partial healing and that is not His plan for us. We may always have remorse about areas of sin that have harmed us or others, but that is different to being bound to the sin and not able to freely heal.

Repentance – a Commandment or a Gift?

As we have discussed throughout the curriculum, we do not rely on feelings or our mind to make a matter true. We have to know in our spirit that something has been established. This is very true when we look at repentance. There are times that we struggle with repentance for a variety of reasons. We may like our sin. It may fill a need, like comfort, justification or fear.

So, what do we do when we don't "feel" like repenting? Just like forgiveness, repentance starts with your will. You make a choice. This choice may be devoid of all emotion, or it may be filled with emotion. What does your spirit say? Are you in relationship with God, without block or hindrance? Are you listening to the voice of shame or is the Holy Spirit bringing conviction because you have not truly laid down the sin at His feet, TURNED AWAY and gone in the other direction? This is where we must cultivate our relationship with the Holy Spirit to clearly hear and heed His voice.

It is the kindness of Jesus that leads us to repentance. *Do you presume on the riches of His kindness and forbearance and patience, not knowing that God's kindness is meant to lead you to repentance?* Romans 2:3-4. This is such a beautiful picture of God's love toward us. It is our act, but it originates in God. It is His gift to us. The Holy Spirit works in us, resulting in work that flows out of us. Left to our flesh we would turn to rebellion and justification. His grace grants repentance.

Those whom I love I rebuke and discipline. So be earnest and repent. Rev 3:19. In a world of "easy grace and seeker sensitive culture", we must realize that repentance is the heart of Jesus. Scripture makes it very clear that repentance is a CHANGE of heart which results in a change of life: Matt 3:8, Acts 26:20 and Ezek 14:6. The believer is to live a life of repentance.

We are to look differently, act differently, and respond differently. Perhaps no greater was this evident than in the areas of repentance and forgiveness, for it is here that we have our hope as believers. There is hope for true and lasting change. There is hope for true healing and freedom. We are truly cut from a different cloth if we so choose to access the threads of truth available to us.

ReWoven - Continuing the Process of Healing

As we know, the enemy is not a creator. He mimics and he counterfeits. As you continue you will become adept at seeing his strategies, spotting the lies more quickly. There are tools that you've learned along the way that are essential to the process. In the next few pages, we will lay out the grid of healing essentials for quick check-ins. If you feel a certain area causing you to stumble, go back to the full chapter and dig in to see what God may reveal to you on the second look. Perhaps now you are ready to look at the design with fresh eyes or to see a knot that you missed before.

Community

We were created for relationship. What does healthy spiritual community look like? It can be tempting to surround ourselves with others who have walked a similar path, whether it be the shared experience of losing a child, addiction, suicide, infertility, divorce or other issues. It is important to gain wisdom from others' experiences. However, it is important that these relationships are holy and trauma bonds are not created from shared grief.

How do you know if this is happening? Is the goal of the relationship or group simply to feel like you are "one of the club," or is the emphasis on walking in truth and healing? Are you constantly proclaiming over yourself that you are a victim of........ (fill in the blank). Are the bonds created based on mutual respect of personhood and boundaries? Is there healing occurring or is there simply commiserating over shared pain? As with everything we've taught, check the fruit.

Offense

You are no longer subject to every plan of the enemy. You can CHOOSE how you respond. Guard your hearts as you seek to continue healing. Do not allow other offenses to mingle with the newly sewn threads of truth you have established.

Humility and Vulnerability

Vulnerability is at the core of all healing. Guard your heart from any notion that "now I have all the answers," or "I have arrived." God will always call us into more of Him, which requires more surrender of self and more holiness. The journey is unto Him. To be with Him and to be like Him. None of us on this side of heaven walk in complete healing in all areas. Positioning your heart to allow Him and only Him to pull the strings is when the most beautiful music is played.

Leaning into the Process

Depending on the level and frequency of the trauma you have experienced, your journey may take significant time. This is not failure. It is the painstaking process of removing lie after lie. But do not be discouraged for one moment. The presence of Jesus can remove damage that would otherwise take years of counseling and self-help meetings. Another important aspect to remember is that unlike the world, we are seeking discipleship at the same time as we are seeking freedom. There will always be new areas for God to prune and refine, just like our healing, which happens layer by layer, thread by thread. The ultimate purpose is to reveal more and more of Christ in Us...the Hope of glory.

In Chapter One we addressed the warp, or the vertical threads. As we end our journey together in Chapter Eight, let's take a look at the horizontal threads which are called the weft. These threads weave over and under, and over and under to bring strength and security to the design. They are then secured into position by the batten. As God painstakingly weaves His truths through our foundation, we too are strengthened and secured. Interestingly, the strongest of all weaving patterns is the *plain weave*. It is not exactly the most exciting name, but alas the concept is so applicable. The plain weave is the SAME on both sides. The design on the front and the back are identical.

As we continue this process of healing, we are all at different places. None of our stories or responses are the same and therefore none of our tapestries are either. Most of us don't expose the backside of our tapestries to those around us. For some the front and backside may not be all that different. Perhaps a stray thread here and there or some colors that don't match, but for most of us the backside may be fraught with knots, mismatched colors and frayed ends. And alas for some, there may be so much unresolved trauma that even the front of the tapestry is yet unrecognizable as something God has touched.

Regardless of where you are, this is a journey. This class serves to shed light on the true and complete healing that is available in Christ. Eight weeks is merely an introduction to your journey. You may need to revisit specific chapters over and over. As you strengthen the muscles of your will and spirit you will begin to see fruit. You will recognize lies sooner, repent faster and begin to give your spirit more and more authority in your life.

While everyone's tapestry is unique, the principles for healing are universal. The same Master Weaver, God, who is never changing, steadfast and loving, the enemy, the accuser / defiler and ourselves, with our strengths and weaknesses. But the tapestry is now on the loom. The framework has been established. Are you ready to allow the Master Designer to continue the process of weaving new truths, strengthening weak threads and perhaps cutting some things away?

You can take these past 8 weeks and skim the surface and have a few key take-away moments, or you can choose to apply the truths in every area of pain and relational turmoil. Yes, the process can be difficult, but the result of true healing is so rewarding. You are worth it.

You are His Masterpiece
You are ReWoven

Perch and Scour

Jesus, as an act of my will, I choose forgiveness of myself, God and others. I know this is a process and at times, I feel as though I'm stuck. I give You permission to soften my heart and bring the gift of repentance into my life in new ways. My desire is to walk in joy and freedom. I recognize that I have a will and I can make choices that hinder or expedite healing. Soften my heart to the move of Your spirit. Minister to my emotions that seem so strong at times. Help me to grow in yielding to the work of the Holy Spirit in all areas of my life so that I may truly know peace.

Father, I need community. I need accountability. I choose vulnerability in this process of healing. I choose to partner with You to see complete healing in my relationships, including my relationship with myself.

You have created me, even in my mother's womb. I am fearfully and wonderfully made. Help me to see the beauty of your creation.

About the Author

Vicki Vibbert has spent 30 years ministering in the areas of inner healing, deliverance and discipleship. As a frequent speaker and ministry facilitator, she combines experience, knowledge and humor to address the depths of pain and bondage of the human experience.

Her favorite role is that of teacher/facilitator, creating space for people to experience the tangible presence of the Holy Spirit as they apply truth to areas of bondage. Vicki is the Executive Director of Tapestry Family Services in Indiana, a domestic adoption agency which also offers a weaving of case management and trauma resources for victims of trauma, including retreats, ministry sessions and classes. Tapestry focuses on bringing wholeness to the mind, body and spirit. Vicki is the adoptive mother of two children, Josiah and Nicole.

ReWoven-Restoring God's Ultimate Design is the first published book in the Tapestry series addressing trauma in the life of the believer.

If you would like further support, please reach out to Vicki Vibbert at vicki@tapestry-adoption.com or phone at: +1 317 529 7322

Made in the USA
Columbia, SC
21 October 2024

44821061R00076